1538

HARDY THE NOVELIST

HARDY THE NOVELIST

An Essay in Criticism

By

DAVID CECIL

THE CLARK LECTURES
given at Cambridge in 1942

*

CONSTABLE AND CO LTD · LONDON

PUBLISHED BY

Constable and Company Ltd.

LONDON

First published   March 1943
Second Impression   April 1943
Third Impression   May 1943
Fourth Impression   September 1943
Fifth Impression   June 1944

Printed in Great Britain by T. and A. CONSTABLE LTD.
at the University Press, Edinburgh

To
ELIZABETH BOWEN

PREFATORY NOTE

THIS study was composed as a course of lectures. I fear that, transferred to the printed page, its mode of expression may seem at once too colloquial and too declamatory, too loose in structure and too emphatic in phrase, not to jar on a fastidious taste. If so, I hope my critics will remember that it was designed to be heard by an audience, not perused by a solitary reader ; and will grant me their indulgence.

May I also take this occasion to thank the Master and Fellows of Trinity College, Cambridge, first for doing me the honour of inviting me to deliver the Clark Lectures, and secondly for the warmth of their welcome to me during my sojourn in their stately courts.

DAVID CECIL.

NEW COLLEGE, OXFORD.

I

HIS SCOPE

CERTAINLY it is gratifying to be asked to deliver the Clark Lectures. Yet, when I first sat down seriously to consider the task before me, gratification changed to despondency. For these lectures meant literary criticism; and, somehow, I found myself disinclined to add to the already formidable bulk of literary criticism. That spirit of disillusionment which, we are told, is characteristic of the present age, had begun, like the thin rays of a winter daybreak, to penetrate the antique seclusion of my College rooms, revealing their contents in a grey and disenchanting light. I examined the rows of critical books which lined my shelves—sound old-fashioned works with titles like "Towards a Theory of Comedy" and "18th Century Influences in Romantic Poetry," or lively modern cantankerous books called "Rhythm as Pattern" and "The Tragedy of Coleridge" —and was filled with a sense of futility. It is true that they were, most of them, ingenious and learned works; and reading them was a pleasant enough occupation. Nor was it more harmful, I dare say, than gazing out of the window and watching the tawny leaves drift and circle one after another down the waters of the River Thames. But it was about as fruitful. For what, after all, was the good of it? How far did all this erudition and industry and ill-temper make any difference to my appreciation of letters? What living connection was there between these books and the feeling stirred in me by reading "Hamlet" or "The Ancient Mariner"? The answer, I am afraid, is that there was very little. The reason that so much criticism is unprofitable is that the critics do not stick to their subject. This subject is books. In every generation certain books are written which are works of art, which we read not for any ulterior motive—not for instruction or edification—but for the same reason that we go to a picture gallery or a concert: because reading them is in itself a satisfying experience. These books are the critic's subject; they are what he starts with, they are the cause and justification of his existence. It is his function to illuminate our appreciation of them, to define the nature of the satisfaction they give, to analyse the circumstances conditioning their production and the arts by which they make their impression. This ought to be enough work for any one man. Critics, however, seldom seem to think so. Instead, they take the opportunity to write about all sorts of other topics—the nature of aesthetics, the political opinions of Shelley, the character of Lord Byron's wife. No wonder we do not find them very helpful. Of course, one can understand why they go astray. Every work of literary art is the result of a double impulse. In the first place, it is an expression of the artist's personal vision. Wordsworth wants to tell us what he feels when he looks at a daisy. But the writer is also actuated by a more purely creative impulse. He wants to make something in a particular medium, to construct a pleasing object in words, as the sculptor wants to construct a pleasing object in stone. Both these impulses are essential ingredients for the creation of any true work of literature. Without the personal impulse the result is only an exercise in conventional pattern writing, like a schoolboy's copy of Latin verses. Without the formal impulse the result is only a raw fragment of autobiography.

Now it is vital that the critic should keep the dual character of his subject in mind; he must stick vigilantly to a central path from which both these aspects are equally visible. If he does not, he will soon stray off his subject altogether. On one side of the road there lies in wait for him the barren uplands of pedantry. The pedantic critic concentrates only on the formal aspect of literature. He theorises on the nature of art in general, lays down laws for tragedy or fiction or style, and then proceeds to judge books by these laws. The consequence is disastrous. Pedantic critics are the people who condemn Shakespeare's tragedies for offending against the three unities; who deny Sir Thomas Browne's right to be called a prose writer on the ground that his eloquence stirs emotions that by their rules should be roused only by verse; who disapprove of Milton's style because he uses a number of Latin words, in their view inadmissible in an English book; who will not allow Whitman to be a poet because he does not write in regular metre. They make these inept statements because they forget that a work of art is the expression of a personal vision and so, to a certain extent, must create its own appropriate form, be judged by its own rules. There are no divine laws of art. What we call laws are tentative generalisations drawn from the contemplation of particular works of art. Tragedies exist before the idea of tragedy. The only test of a book's merit is the effect it makes on the reader. If he is thrilled by Shakespeare's tragedies, in spite of the fact that they offend against the unities, so much the worse for the unities. If Milton by using a Latinised form of English can achieve a unique effect of beauty, a Latinised use of English is perfectly justified. The pedantic critic is so concerned with the abstract conception of literature that he forgets the facts on which that conception is founded; he forgets the books.

On the other side of the path of true criticism lie the steamy swamps in which the so-called personal and psychological critics disport themselves. They envisage a book exclusively as the expression of a man; and in consequence judge it by how far they approve or disapprove of his character and opinions. This leads them to make as great fools of themselves as the pedantic critics. The personal critics have scolded Sterne for being immoral and Thackeray for being moral, have rebuked Tolstoy for preaching too much about Napoleon in his novels and Jane Austen for not mentioning Napoleon in hers. The social and political agitations of the present age have led it to invent a new form of this heresy. A race of critics has arisen who judge a book by how far it expresses what they conceive to be the mind of its period. These people rebuke Charles Lamb for writing in what they call a non-contemporary language. They complain that Mrs. Woolf's novels fail to offer any comment on the significance of modern social changes. They also have forgotten the books. We do not read these authors for their moral virtues or social significance. Many worthless writers would do equally well for that purpose. Moreover, books of equal merit can be written from the most antagonistic point of view and expressing the most diverse views of society. It is here that we should recollect the formal element in the artist's impulse. Certain authors are worthy subjects for literary criticism because they have shown the power to incarnate their vision beautifully in a fitting medium. The satisfaction they give us is its own complete justification. If Jane Austen can write a brilliant and beautifully designed comedy without mentioning the Napoleonic wars she has no need to bother about them. If Lamb's style delights us, let it be as non-contemporary as he pleases.

I do not pretend to be immune from temptations which have overcome other men more eminent than myself. So when I did myself the honour to accept the invitation to deliver these lectures, I made up my mind to formulate their title in such a way as to keep me as strictly as possible in the true path of criticism. I decided to write about a particular author in order to stop myself declaiming in the void about aesthetic theory; and, lest I should begin gossiping about Hardy's relations to Mrs. Hardy, I entitled my course "An

Essay in Criticism." No doubt I shall find myself sometimes straying on to other ground. We cannot understand Hardy without knowing something about his age and his character. And the study of his art will suggest thoughts on the nature of art in general. Still, I shall do my best to admit these topics only in so far as they assist me in my aim, which is to elucidate the nature and quality of his achievement.

If I fail, it will not be the fault of my subject. Hardy is peculiarly appropriate material for such a task. For he stands at the right distance from us. He is still young enough to be fresh. His best work was all written within the last seventy years; he only died in 1928. He has not yet achieved a settled status in English literature. No traditional image of him has yet grown up to obscure our clear and independent view of him. Our judgement is not liable to be blurred by those clouds of orthodox praise and blame that gather round the figure of an established classic.

On the other hand, he is far enough away for us to be able to judge him with detachment. All living writers, says Hazlitt, are our friends or our foes. This is distressingly true. We cannot forget that Mr. Ernest Hemingway, let us say, took an enlightened view of the Spanish war; or that Mr. T. S. Eliot is an Anglo-Catholic and a Royalist. Our judgement of these authors is affected by these considerations. To approach their work in the mood, receptive yet detached, which is essential to the just appreciation of art, is beyond the power of all but the most self-disciplined critic.

We are still more likely to be prejudiced when we are dealing with an author just not contemporary. Each age reacts against its predecessor, generally so violently that all that predecessor's productions, good and bad alike, seem equally offensive to the next generation's taste. Have you ever noticed, when looking at a photographic group taken twenty years ago, that it is impossible to judge which women are well dressed, for all the clothes look equally grotesque; whereas in a group taken forty years ago some were clearly charming? The same phenomenon is true of literature. During the early years of the present century people were in such violent revolt against that Victorian view of life so perfectly expressed by Tennyson, that Tennyson's stock went rushing down. Now that the Victorian age is thoroughly behind us, Tennyson's reputation is once more rising.

Even if we do manage to discipline ourselves sufficiently to withstand these prejudices, it still remains very hard to get a fair view of a relatively recent book. The writer who is a genuine artist is distinguished from the writer who is not by the fact that his creations are imbued with a vitality that does not grow less with time. Steeped in the vital element of Dickens's imagination, Mr. Micawber seems as alive today as on the morning he made his first appearance before the public. But most would-be creative literature is not thus the expression of an individual vision. It merely reflects, more or less successfully, conceptions of the world current in its time. Now, while these conceptions prevail, the literature that reflects them partakes of their vitality. Agnes Wickfield, unlike Mr. Micawber, has no real individuality; she is merely a conventional symbol of the Victorian ideal of womanhood. This did not matter so much to Dickens's first readers. For to them her figure was animated by the vitality of the living ideal of which she was the representative. It is only now, when this ideal is out of date, that we realise what a puppet she is. A certain time must elapse before we can easily separate what is permanent in an artist's work from what is temporary.

For Hardy this time has elapsed. The world he lived in is as much part of vanished history as the world of Queen Elizabeth. The problems that occupied it are either solved or present themselves in a different form. We are no longer his friends or his foes. At last we can without difficulty approach his work in the proper detached, perceptive mood. Further, we can be pretty sure that such of it as now seems vivid will still seem vivid to people a hundred years hence, and that such part as seems faded is faded irretrievably. His figure has receded to a distance in which it can be seen in the same perspective with that of Fielding or Sir Walter Scott, and in which we can discriminate his essential quality with the same impartial clarity. We are in as good a position as we shall ever be to come to a final judgement on him.

Even so, of course, our minds will need a little readjusting before they are ready for the task. First of all, we must acquaint ourselves with his creative range. We have to do this before making a judgement on any novelist. A novel is a work of art in so far as it introduces us into a living world; in some respects resembling the world we live in, but with an individuality of its own. Now this world owes its character to the fact that it is begotten by the artist's creative faculty on his experience. His imagination apprehends reality in such a way as to present us with a new vision of it. But in any one artist only some aspects of his experience fertilise his imagination, strike sufficiently deep down into the fundamentals of his personality to kindle his creative spark. His achievement, therefore, is limited to that part of his work which deals with these aspects of his experience. Only in so far as it stays within their limits does his work have creative life. It is therefore the first duty of a critic to realise this range. Otherwise he will always be looking for something in a book that it does not profess to provide. Many critics, who should know better, do not seem to realise this obligation. They condemn Emily Brontë for not showing us more of the brighter side of life; or Henry James for only writing about the rich. But the brighter side of life did not stimulate Emily Brontë's imagination. Nor was Henry James inspired by the contemplation of impoverished persons. They were therefore quite right to pass them by. If they had tried to write about them, they would have made a dreadful hash of it. For they would have been going outside their range. And to blame a novelist for staying inside his range is as silly as to blame a portrait-painter for not giving us any pictures of trees.

What then was Hardy's range? In the first place, it was conditioned by the circumstances of his early life. This is often so with a writer. The type of life and character to which people are brought up is the only type which they understand instinctively. Their subsequent and mature view of human nature in general is always founded on this, the first example with which they came into contact. Further, most people are intensely receptive to experience only when they are young. It is then that impressions pierce down to that deepest stratum of the mind where the seeds of creative life lie hid. First impressions are the most fundamental and the most durable. Scott, brought up in Edinburgh and the country round it, is most creative when he writes about the people of this district. Conrad's most memorable figures are drawn from the seamen he lived amongst during the impressionable years of his early maturity. Hardy is no exception to this rule. He was the son of humble parents, only just above the rank of labourer, and the first twenty years of his life were spent between the village of Bockhampton, which was his home, and the neighbouring town of Dorchester. Rural Dorset is a remote place, and it was more remote in the early years of the nineteenth century than it is now. Feudal and sequestered, centring round church and village inn and squire's manor house, its life—little touched by the changes of the great world—revolved in the same slow rhythm as for hundreds of years past. It was an agricultural life. Everyone, except the clergyman and the schoolmaster, lived by the land. And they lived hard. In clay-built cramped cottages men struggled year after year against wind and

l mummers' plays, are scattered broadcast ov

er effect of Hardy's environment was to turn
ion towards the past. He was stirred primarily by
he had known as a child, and of his most famous
ly "Tess" and "Jude" deal with the contemporary
his mature years; the rest are set in the world of
hood. This world in its turn was closely linked
nore ancient history. Wessex life was too un-
, too uneventful, for people to forget the past.
ttage, every landmark was thick with survivals and
s of history. And Wessex has played a large part
y. The primitive inhabitants of this island had
the Downs with their barrows. The men of the
Ages had built churches there; the Elizabethans had
culptured manor houses; Cavalier and Roundhead
ht in the fields and hidden in the woods. And, in
ent times, the armies of England had gathered there
the invasion of Napoleon. Hardy was acutely
to the picturesque appeal of the past. As a matter
he himself came of an ancient local family, more
s once than it was now. A Thomas Hardy of the
century founded the Dorchester Grammar School;
esses of Dorchester had put up a tablet to him
mend to Posterity an example so worthy of imita-
more famous Hardy had bent in the dark tumbling
he *Victory* to catch the last words of the dying
Some of the stories that caught our Hardy's fancy
child were anecdotes of his forebears. His mother's
, so the legend ran, had sheltered Monmouth after
of Sedgemoor. He made a short story out of this,
ike's Reappearance." He wrote several historical
ries and one novel, "The Trumpet Major." But
modern books, too, are resonant with echoes of an
e. The Casterbridge of which Henchard is Mayor

weather to support a wife and family on 7s. a week. But it had stability and dignity. Every Sunday in the grey old churches the community met together, as their ancestors had done for generations, to hear their joys and sorrows voiced and sanctified in the sublime meditations of Prayer-Book and Authorised Version. It had its light relief too, home-made traditional pleasures — harvest celebrations, Christmas gaieties, parties to celebrate birth and marriage —where people danced and sang ballads and drank cider and told stories. Hardy's father was a musician, famous in the neighbourhood. His son took after him. At eleven years old he would go off to fiddle at a wedding party or a Christmas party. Until two in the morning he would play sometimes, bowing away indefatigably while the couples wove their way through the figures of the country dances. And then, so he tells us in his recollections, would come a pause when the girls, clustered together in their light gowns against the wall in the barn, would warble a traditional ballad:

> "Lie there, lie there, thou false-hearted man,
>   Lie there instead o' me;
> For six pretty maidens thou hast a'drowned here,
>   But the seventh hath drown-ed thee!"

Tragedy was not confined to ballads. Real life had its drama too at Bockhampton: strange simple dramas arising from the narrow poverty-stricken circumstances in which its inhabitants lived. Lovers were parted: a young man, in need of a livelihood, would leave the place to seek his fortune; years later he would return, to find his sweetheart married to another. In such a world, confined and elemental, passions grew to obsessions. Men, brooding on their wrongs until they seemed intolerable, found vent for their emotion in crime. Then, by the stern laws of those days, the offenders would be hanged at Dorchester. Hardy saw two hangings before he was eighteen. He stood under the scaffold to see a woman die on one occasion. On another, from a neighbouring hill, he watched through a telescope the white figure of a man, silhouetted against the façade of the prison, drop down from the gallows as the clock struck eight. Overcome with horror, he turned homeward.

He was a very sensitive boy, responding precociously to experience; and the life in which he grew up stamped itself so deeply on his imagination that, when his faculties had reached the creative stage of development, he conceived his picture of life in its terms. The most living part of his work is always concerned with it, and it is responsible for some of its most characteristic features. Nature, first of all, played a larger part in his books than in those of any other English novelist. It is not just the background in his drama, but a leading character in it. Sometimes it exercises an active influence on the course of events: more often it is a spiritual agent, colouring the mood and shaping the disposition of human beings. The huge bleak darkness of Egdon Heath dominates the lives of the characters in "The Return of the Native," infusing into them its grandeur and its melancholy; the solitary wistfulness of the woods is the keynote of sentiment of "The Woodlanders" who lived among them. As its title suggests, the distinctive mark of the characters in Hardy's second novel comes from the fact that they dwell "under the greenwood tree." His most living characters, moreover, are always natives of the countryside. Farmers and shepherds, thatchers and hedgers, they, most of them, never stray beyond its borders. A few, indeed, go off as soldiers or sailors, like the Loveday brothers in "The Trumpet Major"; very rarely one with exceptional intellectual aspirations, like Clym Yeobright or Jude Fawley, will depart to seek fulfilment in a higher sphere. But soldiers and intellectuals alike remain countrymen still. However much they travel or educate themselves, they bear the stamp of field and village on every facet of their person-

alities. Out of their original enviro...
Indeed, so far as the motives actuati...
not motives of rural life, they turn o...
rural circumstances and the aspiratio...
confined in them towards a more r...
longs to satisfy his desire for learnin...
for the colour and luxury of life in F...
hesitate to marry their rustic sweeth...
of the great world has made their ta...

For the plots of Hardy's books a...
by his upbringing as are his settin...
comedy turns on the genial, farcica...
His tragedy is village tragedy, co...
broken love and wronged girls, the...
which filled his early memories. A...
their mark too. There is always s...
about Hardy's plots. They are full...
maidens and dashing Don Juans. ...
is a ballad tale of the pretty gi...
between handsome soldier and g...
in "Far From the Madding Cr...
figure of the dashing, inconstant s...
town, who kisses and rides away. ...
so modern and advanced in its da...
peeled of its realistic trappings, ...
folk-tale tragedy. Tess, the be...
betrayed by a wicked seducer ...
gallows tree. Hardy's stories a...
popular superstition which pla...
histories he listened to round ...
evenings—the witchcraft and ...
Return of the Native," the mid...
sought to divine the name of the...
and "The Woodlanders"; ...
ceremonies and gaieties, carol-...

B

is ancient Casterbridge, with its Georgian houses and Gothic churches and, outside the limit of the old rampart, a huge prehistoric earthwork. Tess—we are not likely to forget it! —is a descendant of the ancient family of d'Urberville, with their heraldic tombs in the church of Kingsbere. When Jude goes to Christminster, he walks the streets hardly able to see the modern scene for the crowding spectres of the ancient worthies of the University. The great houses of Wessex, standing aloof from the villages, in their stately parks, are also landmarks in Hardy's landscape. The thought of their owners was romantic to him, and stirred him to compose imaginary tales about their lives—"Two on a Tower," "A Group of Noble Dames." He was fascinated by the idea of heredity. He loved to trace the family type continuous through generations. This is the theme of "The Well-Beloved"; it is an important element in that of "Tess." He delights equally to perceive the mark of the past in humbler spheres; to show how the feet of its ancient inhabitants have worn the paving-stones of Miller Loveday's kitchen; to preserve in his pages the memory of some traditional occupation now growing obsolete, like that of the reddleman in "The Return of the Native."

Hardy's range, then, is limited, in the first place, by the circumstances of his upbringing. It is further defined by his angle of vision. Like that of other novelists, Hardy's subject is human life. But human life can be looked at from many aspects and in many relations. Hardy regards it in its most fundamental aspect. He sees human beings less as individuals than as representatives of a species, and in relation to the ultimate conditioning forces of their existence. His subject is not men, but man. His theme is mankind's predicament in the universe.

As seen by him, it is a tragic theme. The world he lived in had something to do with this. There was plenty of tragedy in the life of the Wessex labourer, with its poverty and its passion. Life to them was life in the raw. Dependent and ignorant, exposed alike to the oppressions of the social system and the caprice of the weather, at every moment of their existence the people among whom Hardy was brought up were made conscious of man's helplessness in the face of circumstances. Hardy, too, was the man to realise the tragedy implicit in such a life. He had a tender heart, unusually responsive to the spectacle of suffering. As a little boy, he even hated seeing the boughs lopped off the trees; the first time he saw a dead bird he was struck by an appalling, unforgettable chill of horror. By the time he was fifteen a shadow had already fallen across his vision of life. He tells us he remembers lying back in the sun and wishing that he need not grow up. He wanted to stay just as he was, in the same place, with the same few friends. The infinite possibilities mature life seemed to hold for failure and for suffering appalled him, and made him shrink back into such security as he already knew. This shrinking from life embodied itself in the form of spectral fear. He fancied, he says, "that a figure stood in his van, with arm uplifted, to knock him back from any pleasant prospect he indulged in as probable." And not only him. It was the enemy of mankind in general. For Hardy's was a speculative mind, instinctively reasoning from particular observations to a general conclusion. Since the world he looked at seemed so full of pain and disappointment, then, he argued, pain and disappointment were outstanding characteristics of human existence.

This disposition to a melancholy view was confirmed and increased by the age in which he lived. It was a disturbing age for a sensitive mind; for it was an age of transition. The industrial revolution was in the process of destroying the old agricultural England; the population was shifting; the old ties which had united the small communities of the past were breaking bit by bit. Along with the disintegration of the old social and economic structure went a disintegration of ideas. Eighteenth-century rationalism had united with the new romantic spirit of rebellion against convention, to shake the fundamental basis of belief—religious, social, political—which the people of the old England had unquestioningly accepted. Since the beginning of the century, leaders of thought were, more often than not, unorthodox. The mental atmosphere of reflective minds tended to be overcast by clouds of doubt. Toward the middle of the century it was further disturbed by the higher criticism of the Bible and the Darwinian theory of evolution. People were feeling already uncertain about the philosophic basis of Christianity. Now they began to doubt the historical facts on which that philosophy rested. And not only Christianity—the new ideas struck a blow at all religious and ideal interpretations of the universe. If, as seemed possible, it was only a mechanical process, evolving from no one knew what, in a direction no one knew whither, what was the significance of those moral and spiritual values which man had learned to regard as the most precious things in life? If Christianity was not true, what became of the consolation of Christianity, the conception of Divine justice, bringing all to good in the end? New thinkers—some rationalist, some romantic—disputed vaguely and acrimoniously with one another as to what creed should take the place of the old religious certainty. None of their alternatives proved sufficiently convincing to establish itself unquestioned in men's minds, as the old faith had done. The thoughtful person saw himself swept upwards from darkness to darkness, like a straw on a torrent, by a ruthless, mysterious and ignoble force. Artists, always peculiarly sensitive to the atmosphere of their environment, were affected by this atmosphere of doubt and apprehension. Some, supported by personal religious experience, still discovered fresh

strength in the old faith. Others took refuge in worlds of
beauty conjured up by their imaginations. But there were
those who could find no such consolation for themselves;
and, for the first time, pessimism—conscious, considered
pessimism—found expression in English letters: in the
works of Arnold and FitzGerald, of Thompson and Hardy.
Hardy was especially open to the melancholy implications
of the new outlook. As a countryman, he belonged to the
world that was passing. That rural England, which was
hallowed for him by every tie of childish sentiment, was
beginning to crumble before his eyes. Every year he noticed
that old habits were discontinued; that stories and songs
were being forgotten; that families established for years in
a place were leaving it. No doubt the standard of living was
improving, but against any satisfaction this might bring to
his moral sense was balanced his regret at the passing of
what had seemed so secure. The most established institutions seemed precarious; life seemed precarious too.

He was still more affected by the disintegration of the old
ideas. Brought up in a society in which the tradition of
mediaeval Christianity had lingered longest, he was indelibly
marked by that tradition. His aesthetic sensibility had
found its first satisfaction in the ritual of the Anglican
Church, in the eloquence of Scripture and the venerable
fantasy of the Gothic style. Instinctively he reverenced the
Christian ideal of virtue, above all, he took for granted
the Christian view of the supreme importance of each
individual human being. But there was nothing of the
mystic about Hardy. He had no personal sense of a spiritual
world to support him against the attacks of rationalist critics
on Christian doctrine. His intellect found their arguments
unanswerable. By the age of twenty-seven he had already
lost his faith. He did not feel it a dead loss. Such elements
in Christian morality as were, in Hardy's view, the cause
of suffering—indissoluble marriage, for instance—were, he

thought, a good riddance. And he was angry, a little unreasonably, with the clergy and other orthodox persons who felt it their duty to defend them. Like many village people, Hardy was always ready to grumble about the vicar. But, taken as a whole, he felt that the loss to human happiness involved by the new scientific interpretation of life far outweighed the gain. He felt a wistful yearning for the comfort and the beauty of the old belief:

> "That with this bright believing band
>   I have no claim to be,
> That faiths by which my comrades stand
>   Seem phantasies to me,
> And mirage-mists their Shining Land,
>   Is a strange destiny.
>
> I am like a gazer who should mark
>   An inland company
> Standing upfingered, with 'Hark! hark!
>   The glorious distant sea!'
> And feel, 'Alas, 'tis but yon dark
>   And wind-swept pine to me?'"

Moreover, Hardy did not feel that any of those new philosophies of life which people were constructing to harmonise with the new scientific knowledge could satisfy the heart as Christianity had done. It would have been no use preaching to him of the delights of a world organised to make use of every resource that science had put at man's command. To Hardy, moulded by a religious mode of thought, mere material improvement would not satisfy the demands of man's soul. As for the Nietzschean view that man should be ruthless, like the forces which rule his universe, Hardy thought it both silly and disgusting. No sane man could accept an ideal that went against what instinct told him were the finest feelings of his nature. At one time, Hardy tried to comfort himself with the idea that the universe might, in the course of time, evolve a moral sense. Man had grown more humane through the centuries, so far as one could tell. Might not the cosmos, of which he formed a part, do the same? This whimsical fancy cast a feeble flickering gleam of hope round the close of his great historical drama, "The Dynasts." But he discarded it soon afterwards. The war of 1914 blew its last shreds away. Anyway, it had only been a sporadic flash. His philosophy, from the time he began to write, was confirmedly gloomy. The universe was a huge impersonal mechanism, directed by some automatic principle of life unknown, pursuing its mysterious end, utterly indifferent to the feelings of mortals.

Poor, harassed mankind is not likely to be cheered up by such a view of his existence. "It is better," says Swithin in "Two on a Tower," "for men to forget the universe than to bear it clearly in mind." Hardy agreed with him. But he did not think it possible for man to maintain himself in a state of blessed forgetfulness. If what science said were true, gradually everyone would find it out. Man had reached a stage in his history at which, realising that the old comforting myths were false, he must, for the first time, learn to face the prospect of a life without ultimate hope. This was, to Hardy, a fact of supreme importance, a moment-ous turning-point in the history of mankind. He thought it would modify human nature profoundly. Men would grow to care less for physical beauty; what was physical beauty but a mockery in a world wasting hourly to decay?

"Fair prospects wed happily with fair times; but alas, if times be not fair! Men have oftener suffered from the mockery of a place too smiling for their reason than from the oppression of surroundings over-sadly tinged. Haggard Egdon appealed to a subtler and scarcer instinct, to a more recently learnt emotion, than that which responds to the sort of beauty called charming and fair!

Indeed, it is a question if the exclusive reign of this orthodox beauty is not approaching its last quarter. The new Vale of Tempe may be a gaunt waste in Thule: human souls may find themselves in closer and closer harmony with external things wearing a sombreness distasteful to our race when it was young. The time seems near, if it has not actually arrived, when the chastened sublimity of a moor, a sea, or a mountain will be all of nature that is absolutely in keeping with the moods of the more thinking among mankind."

Nor would man be able to get much satisfaction from knowledge, from the observation and accumulation of facts. "Material fact has ceased to be of importance in art," he says somewhere. "It is the style of a period when the mind is serene and unawakened to the tragical mysteries of life." The new outlook will leave its mark on man's very appearance. Hardy is curiously fascinated by the idea of a new face; a face, he felt, that was appearing in the world as an expression of man's realisation of his sorry predicament. He describes it most fully in his portrait of Clym in "The Return of the Native."

"In Clym Yeobright's face could be dimly seen the typical countenance of the future. Should there be a classic period to art hereafter, its Pheidias may produce such faces. The view of life as a thing to be put up with, replacing that zest for existence which was so intense in early civilizations, must ultimately enter so thoroughly into the constitution of the advanced races that its facial expression will become accepted as a new artistic departure."

This idea of the new man of the future haunted his imagination. It comes into several of his poems and finds its most extreme embodiment in the queer figure of Jude's illegitimate child, Little Father Time . . . the little boy who was born already disillusioned with the world in which he found himself. "I should like the flowers very much," he says, "if I did not keep on thinking they would all be withered in a few days."

The law of nature, cruel and indifferent, forms the background of every one of Hardy's books, incarnating itself now as savage Egdon Heath, now as the woods of Hintock, whose apparent peace masks an unending struggle for survival. Even a love scene, in the pastoral idyll of "Under the Greenwood Tree," is jarred by the anguished scream of a bird caught by an owl. Incidentally, it may be noted that Hardy's melancholy philosophy increased the disposition, implanted by his environment, to place his scene in the peasant world of his youth. There, he remembered, people were still untouched by the disturbing influences of modern thought. There they were still blessedly unaware of the true grimness of the human predicament. The most characteristic note in all Hardy's emotional scale—the strain which, as it were, forms an accompanying undercurrent alike to his scenes of fun and his scenes of tragedy—its nostalgia; the longing for a world where, if happiness were not really attainable, men were still under the illusion that it could be attained. Nostalgia, gentle in "Under the Greenwood Tree," lyrical in "The Woodlanders," romantic in "The Trumpet Major," bitter in "Jude," echoes hauntingly through his every work.

A struggle between man on the one hand and, on the other, an omnipotent and indifferent Fate—that is Hardy's interpretation of the human situation. Inevitably it imposes a pattern on his picture of the human scene. It determines the character of his drama. Like other dramas, this turns on a conflict; but the conflict is not, as in most novels, between one man and another, or between man and an institution. Man in Hardy's books is ranged against impersonal forces, the forces conditioning his fate. Not that his characters themselves are always aware of this. Henchard is obsessed by his hatred of Farfrae; Bathsheba looks on Troy as the author of her misfortunes. But from the point of vantage from which Hardy surveys their stories,

Bathsheba and Henchard are seen to be under a delusion. For those whom they think their enemies are as much as themselves puppets in the hand of Fate. Fate, not them, is ultimately responsible for their quarrels. Unless they were destined to do so, they would not be in conflict with each other. Not that Hardy refuses to make moral distinctions between his characters. On the contrary, his leading figures divide themselves into instruments for good and instruments for evil. The line between them is determined by their attitude to themselves. All alike are striving for happiness; but whereas Eustacia or Fitzpiers or Arabella strive with selfish passion, Gabriel and Tess and Giles are prepared to sacrifice their own happiness to ensure that of other people. This difference, however, in their characters does not affect the issue. That is in the hands of Fate. And indeed it is significant that Hardy—as a rule—emphasises the fact that even those characters the world would call wicked are so much the creatures of circumstance that they are far more to be pitied than to be blamed. Henchard, for instance, seems, on the face of it, faulty enough—violent, vindictive and uncontrolled. From that first chapter in which he sells his wife at the Fair, until the end of the story, when he deliberately conceals from Elizabeth-Jane the news of her father's arrival, lest she should wish to leave him, he acts in such a way as to justify an old-fashioned orthodox moralist in condemning him as the architect of his own misfortunes. But Hardy does not look at him in this way. Henchard, as he sees him, is a pathetic figure, born with an unfortunate disposition but genuinely longing to do right, tortured by remorse when he does wrong, and always defeated by some unlucky stroke of Fate. Eustacia too— the gorgeous, tragic Eustacia of "The Return of the Native" —what desolation she brings on all around her in her un- scrupulous fight for happiness! Yet Hardy does not represent her as hateful. An exotic orchid, planted by chance in the unfriendly northern moorland of Egdon, who can condemn her for snatching at every chance to achieve the sort of life in which alone her nature can find fulfilment? She has no wish to make other people unhappy; only, forced by the pressure of her nature towards the sunlight, she brushes aside anything that impedes her way. Fate is her enemy, as it is that of her rivals. In a just vision of human life, all men alike are seen as brothers, banded against untoward Fate.

Fate is an abstraction, and in order that it may play an active part in a human drama, it must be personified in some particular incarnation. This necessity also determines the nature of Hardy's drama. Hardy embodies Fate in various forms. Sometimes it appears as a natural force. Henchard's plans for making himself rich are brought to nought by a bad harvest; the weather takes the part of Fate here. Sometimes it embodies itself as some innate weakness of character. Jude's life is ruined because he has been endowed at birth, through no wish of his own, with an intensity of sexual temperament which he cannot control, and which is his undoing. Chiefly, however, the forces of Fate in Hardy's novels incarnate themselves in two guises— as chance, and as love. Of these, chance is the most typical. In no other novels does chance exercise such a conspicuous influence on the course of events. Hardy has been blamed for this: and no doubt he does sometimes overdo it. But to condemn his use of chance altogether is to misunderstand his view of life. We are witnessing a battle between man and Destiny. Destiny is an inscrutable force; we do not understand its nature or its intentions. And we cannot therefore predict what it will do. In consequence, its acts always show themselves in the guise of inexplicable, un- expected blows of chance. Mrs. Yeobright calls on a visit of reconciliation with her son at the one moment when, by an unlucky combination of circumstances, Eustacia, his

wife, cannot admit her. In consequence, she goes away
to die, unreconciled with him. This is not just a mere
clumsy device to make the story end sadly. Hardy is out to
show that Mrs. Yeobright and Eustacia, in their struggle for
happiness, are alike up against the process of the universal
plan, which takes no account of their feelings and may therefore make a move—from pure caprice, it may seem—which
renders their efforts vain. Such apparent accidents are
really as typical an expression of the nature of Fate as
Mrs. Yeobright's wish to make up her quarrel with her son
is an expression of her nature.

Always, so Hardy tells us, there is discord in the nature
of existence. Man is working to one end, Destiny to
another. These ends may coincide or they may not. Either
way, it is Destiny who decides what shall happen. Man
cannot modify the will of Destiny. It is significant how
many of Hardy's plots turn on the revelation of a past action
coming to light after being kept secret for some time. This
happens in "A Pair of Blue Eyes," "Far from the Madding
Crowd," "The Return of the Native," "The Mayor of
Casterbridge" and "Tess." No doubt this was a common
device in the stories of the period, as it has been a common
device since stories were first invented. But Hardy charges
it with a graver import than most authors. For by this means
he can convey how the fate of his characters is predetermined
by forces hidden from them. To the characters, the past
may be dead; they may have put their past actions behind
them. But they cannot escape their consequences. For
the action has become a hostage which they have presented
to Destiny and which Destiny may use against them, which
it will use with a ruthless indifference to their feelings, if it
should prove necessary to its mysterious purpose.

These past actions are all connected with love. This
brings me to the second form in which Hardy chiefly
incarnates Fate. All Hardy's novels are love stories Love

is the predominating motive actuating his characters. Once
or twice he presents us with a hero moved by other desires:
Jude longs for learning; Swithin is ruled by his passion
for astronomy. But Swithin's story soon becomes a love
story; and before we are a third through Jude's history he
has forgotten his intellectual ambitions and is absorbed
solely in his passion for Sue. Indeed, it is very natural
that love should dominate Hardy's scene. Man, cast into
a dark and unsatisfying world, thirsts for happiness. The
happiness promised by love is the most universal symbol
of this thirst that Hardy could have chosen. For every sort
of human being in every sort of circumstance responds to
the call of love; in love's ecstasy they find an intimation
of the happiness that they hope will free them from the
burden of the human lot. Alas, their hope is vain. For love,
so far from being a benevolent spirit, consoling and helping
man in his struggle with the inhuman forces controlling
human existence, is itself a manifestation of these forces.
Love, conceived by Hardy, is "the Lord of terrible aspect"
—a blind, irresistible power, seizing on human beings
whether they will or not; intoxicating in its inception, but,
more often than not, bringing ruin in its train. His men and
women would find it possible to walk the bleak road from
the cradle to the grave resignedly enough; they might
endure life fairly easily, even if they did not enjoy it, were
it not for this storm which sweeps them off their feet, only
to fling them down again, broken and despairing. Even in
"The Trumpet Major" or "Far from the Madding Crowd,"
when love does achieve a happy fruition, it is shadowed with
sadness. It is a minor key, twilight serenity, that closes the
drama of Bathsheba and Gabriel; Anne and Bob Loveday
may be happy, but their happiness is won at the expense
of John, the noblest of the three. "Under the Greenwood
Tree" is the only one of Hardy's successful works in which
the love story ends in unqualified sunshine, and "Under

the Greenwood Tree" is the light-weight among his master-pieces. In all the other great works, love shows itself nakedly—a beautiful and baleful God.

With this emphasis on love goes an emphasis on the part played by women in the human drama. To Hardy, as to Byron, love was women's whole existence. Indeed, he had what is, rightly or wrongly, called "the old-fashioned view of women." He stresses their frailty, their sweetness, their submissiveness, their coquetry, their caprice. Even when they are at fault, he represents them with a tender chivalry. Arabella in "Jude" is the only odious woman in Hardy's books. And "Jude" was written in a mood of bitterness unique in Hardy's work. For the most part, Hardy treats women with sympathy; the sufferings of Tess, of Elfride, of Marty, of Bathsheba, are touched with a peculiar pathos. This, no doubt, was partly due to the bias of Hardy's temperament; he was a born lover of the sex. But it, too, is a consequence of his view of the human predicament. Woman's passiveness and frailty make her an especially poignant illustration of that frailty, that dependence on fate, which is the outstanding characteristic of the human lot. Fate, it is true, often employs a human instrument to en-compass the tragedies which overtake Hardy's heroines. Tess and Bathsheba, Thomasin and Grace are the victims of Don Juans. Angel and Swithin and Knight inflict un-merited suffering on the women they love from a harsh, doctrinaire idealism that freezes the flow of natural com-passion. Hardy's strong natural human sympathy makes him particularly hostile to such idealism. But, as we have seen, he does not lay the chief responsibility for human suffering on human beings. Knight and Troy and the rest of them are instruments. Tess and Elfride are repre-sentatives of mankind, eternally and always the victim of superhuman forces.

They gain in stature from this vaster significance which

Hardy attaches to them. Indeed—and this is the final effect of his philosophy on his work—the angle from which he surveyed human life was such as to make his picture of it drawn on the grandest scale. We are shown life in its fundamental elements, as exemplified by simple, elemental characters, actuated by simple, elemental passions. What others exhibit man's ultimate relation to Destiny? And the fact that they are seen in relation to ultimate Destiny gives them a gigantic and universal character. Nor is the universality of this picture weakened by the fact that Hardy writes only of country people in nineteenth-century Wessex. On the contrary, he preferred this setting because he thought that in such a society human existence appeared at its most elemental, with its naked structure unconcealed by the superficial trappings of more sophisticated modes of existence. Concentrated in this narrow, sequestered form of life, the basic facts of the human drama showed up at their strongest; undisturbed by other distractions, the basic human passions burned at their hottest.

"It was one of those sequestered spots," he says, describing the hamlet of Hintock, which is the centre of the tragical history of "The Woodlanders,"

"outside the gates of the world where may usually be found more meditation than action, and more listlessness than meditation; where reasoning proceeds on narrow premises, and results in inferences wildly imaginative; yet where, from time to time, dramas of a grandeur and unity truly Sophoclean are enacted in the real, by virtue of the concentrated passions and closely knit interdependence of the lives therein."

So might he have spoken of all his stories. For all that Hardy makes such play with the local characteristics of his scene, yet always he penetrates beneath them to those universal facts of human existence of which this scene is only one example. In spite of the loving exactitude with which he details the characteristic features of Wessex life, he never lets us forget that this Wessex life is part of the life of the whole human race and is inextricably connected with it. I quote once more from "The Woodlanders":

> "Hardly anything could be more isolated or more self-contained than the lives of these two walking here in the lonely hour before day, when grey shades, material and mental, are so very grey. And yet their lonely courses formed no detached design at all, but were part of the pattern in the great web of human doings then weaving in both hemispheres from the White Sea to Cape Horn."

The scale of Hardy's drama is as vast as its setting is confined.

II

HIS POWER

I

HARDY'S imaginative range, then, covers the struggle of mankind with Destiny as exemplified by life in the humbler ranks of a rural society, now specifically the society of early nineteenth-century Wessex. Compared with that of some great novelists, this is a limited range. The theatre of Hardy's drama is built on the grandest scale, but it is sparsely furnished. His range does not allow him to present the vast, varied panorama of human life that we find in "War and Peace" or "L'Education Sentimentale." His scene is too narrow. Many people in the world are not Wessex countrymen, and many of the most important types of people; statesmen, for example, or artists, or philosophers, or men of the world. You will not find these people in Hardy's books. Nor do you find any account of the sort of worlds in which they live. The subtleties of intellectual life, the complexities of public life, the sophistications of social life, these do not kindle Hardy's imagination to work. In fact, it is no good going to him for a picture of the finer shades of civilised life or of the diversity of the human scene as a whole. The life he portrays is life reduced to its basic elements. People in Hardy's books are born, work hard for their living, fall in love and die: they do not do anything else. Such a life limits in its turn the range of their emotions. There is comedy in Hardy's books, and poetry and tragedy; but his comedy is limited to the humours of rustic life, his poetry is the poetry of the folk-song, his tragedy is the stark and simple tragedy of the poor.

The limits imposed by his scene are increased by those of the perspective in which he sees them. After all, only a very few situations illustrate man's relation to the universal plan. There are many other facets of human nature besides those which appear in the conflict of mankind with Fate. Let us imagine a typical figure of man, let us call him John Brown. In addition to Hardy's John Brown—a soul facing the universe—there is also John Brown the citizen, John Brown the Englishman, Jack the family man, John the friend, Brown the member of a profession and Mr. Brown the snob.

Hardy's appreciation of the basic human character enables him to give some account of Jack the family man, his sense of the past reveals to him something of John Brown the Englishman ; though even these aspects of John Brown's nature he portrays only in summary outline. But of the others—the citizen, the professional man, the snob—he gives us nothing at all. For, seen in the terrific perspective in which Hardy surveys the human being, man's struggles as a political and social character seem too insignificant to fire his creative spark. Compared with his relation to the nature of the universe, his relation to government and social systems dwindles to such infinitesimal proportions as to be invisible. And the working of the individual consciousness seems equally insignificant. How can we bother, when we are watching mankind's life-and-death struggle with Fate, to examine the process of the individual's private thought and feeling with the elaborate introspectiveness of Henry James or Proust?

Indeed, Hardy—and here he is very different from almost every other great novelist—does not put his chief stress on individual qualities. As I have said, he writes about man, not about men. Though his great characters are distinguished one from another clearly enough, their individual qualities are made subsidiary to their typical human qualities. And as their stories increase in tension, so do his characters tend to shed individual differences and to assume the impersonal majesty of a representative of all mankind. Giles stands for all faithful lovers, Tess for all betrayed women, Eustacia for all passionate imprisoned spirits.

Hardy's characters linger in our imagination as grand typical figures silhouetted against the huge horizon of the universe. Here they resemble characters of epic and tragedy. Indeed, alike in his themes and his treatment of them, Hardy has less in common with the typical novelist than with the typical author of tragedy and epic. And we must adjust our mental eye to envisage life in the tragic and epic focus if we are to see his vision in the right perspective.

II

We are assisted to do this by the convention he adopts. For our preparations for judging him are not complete when we have realised his range. We must also acquaint ourselves with the conventions within which he elected to compose his pictures. We should in criticising any writer. Every artist constructs his work within certain conventions, which we must accept before we are in a position to estimate his success. Some of the most famous ineptitudes of criticism are due to a failure to realise this obligation. Macaulay read Racine without understanding the conventions of French classical tragedy; he expected all good tragedies to be like Shakespeare's. The consequence was that Racine's subtle and passionate presentation of the drama of the human heart struck him as intolerably stilted and artificial. Voltaire, on the other hand, read Shakespeare's plays expecting them to be like Racine's. He thought, therefore, that Shakespeare was a barbarian. That two persons of this eminence should talk such nonsense should be a warning to the ordinary reader to be careful to acquaint himself with an author's convention before starting to criticise him. He should be particularly careful with Hardy. For Hardy does not write in the convention that one might expect.

Hardy's convention was that of an earlier age, the convention invented by Fielding. The novel is a new form, as forms go, and it was some time before it discovered the convention most appropriate to its matter. It aimed at giving a realistic picture of actual life. How was this to be given a shapely form? Various writers experimented to solve the problem in various ways. Defoe put his tales in the form of autobiography, Richardson in the form of a correspondence. Fielding, who had begun his career as a dramatist, turned to the drama for help. The English novel, as created by Fielding, descends directly from the English drama. Now, that drama was unrealistic. In Shakespeare's day it did not even try to be realistic. It aimed at entertaining its audiences by showing them a world as little like their own as possible: a world in which heroic and dramatic personages took part in picturesque, sensational adventures. The writers of Restoration comedy modified this convention a little. They set their scene in contemporary England and made their characters talk in something approaching the language of real conversation. But essentially their plays remained unrealistic; their plots were highly artificial, their dialogue stiff with ornament and their characters stylised.

Bred to this tradition, Fielding and his followers took for granted that a mere accurate chronicle of ordinary life would be intolerably dull to the reader. So they evolved a working compromise. The setting and characters of their stories were carefully realistic, but they were fitted into a framework of non-realistic plot derived from the drama, consisting of an intrigue enlivened by all sorts of sensational events—conspiracies, children changed at birth, mistakes of identity—centring round a handsome ideal hero and heroine and a sinister villain, and solved neatly in the last chapter. As in the drama, the characters revealed themselves mainly through speech and action—there is not much analysis of them by the author—and the serious tension is relieved by a number of specifically comic characters drawn in a convention of slight caricature.

In one respect this type of novel was even more limited than the drama had been. It was intended as light reading. It might point a moral—it generally did—but it did not deal with those profounder and more impersonal aspects of life which were the subject of serious poetry. It was not supposed to be an intellectual strain, and themes that would set its reader's intellect seriously to work were, except in a few instances, avoided.

This convention was a loose makeshift affair. But it proved less clumsy and more effective than any other hitherto proposed. And, though it gradually discarded its more artificial devices, some elements at least of it were accepted by most English novelists until the time of George Eliot. She was a revolutionary in her sober way. In her books we are presented for the first time with a form of fiction freed from the last vestiges of the dramatic tradition —novels without romantic heroes and villains, with lengthy analysis of motive and character, and in which action is determined by no conventions of plot, but solely by the logical demands of character and situation. In addition, George Eliot, extremely intellectual and uncompromisingly serious, employed her books to expound her most considered reflections on human conduct.

The next generation of novelists carried this change still further. With Henry James, Meredith and George Moore, the novel showed itself as fully entered on a new phase.

Now, Hardy has been looked on usually as part of this new phase. It is natural. For one thing, he was the contemporary of the new novelists; and for another, his books do have some elements in common with theirs. Intellectually, Hardy was a man of the new age—a so-called advanced thinker, in open rebellion against traditional orthodox views about religion, sex and so on—and he used his novels to preach these heretical opinions. Drawing his inspiration largely, as we have seen, from his vision of man's relation to ultimate Fate, he welcomed the movement to deepen and elevate the subject-matter of the novel. Since he wanted to write about tragic and epic subjects, he was pleased that the novel should be regarded as a form capable of achieving tragic and epic dignity. Enthusiastically he discarded the happy ending and made his stories the mouthpieces of his most serious views.

But although intellectually Hardy was a man of the future, aesthetically he was a man of the past. His broad conception of the novel form was much more like that of Fielding than it was like that of Henry James. Circumstances were partly responsible for this. His taste in story-telling was that of the simple rural society in which he had been brought up. He liked a story to be a story. It should have a beginning and an end. It should be full of action. And, above all, it should be sufficiently unusual to arouse the interest of its hearers. It is significant that his first novel, "Desperate Remedies," is prefaced by a quotation from Scott: "Though an unconnected course of adventure is what most frequently occurs in nature, yet, the province of the romance writer being artificial, there is more required from him than a mere compliance with the simplicity of reality." In some scattered notes Hardy expanded the same thesis:

"The recent school of novel writers forget in their insistence on life, and nothing but life, in a plain slice, that a story must be worth the telling, that a good deal of life is not worth any such thing, and that they must not occupy a reader's time with what he can get at first hand anywhere around him."

"A story must be exceptional enough to justify its telling. We tale-tellers are all Ancient Mariners, and none of us is warranted in stopping Wedding Guests (in other words, the hurrying public) unless he has something more unusual to relate than the ordinary experience of every average man and woman."

There was also a more serious motive in his adopting the old convention. It harmonised with the peculiar nature of his inspiration. The presentation of any special vision of reality must involve a process of elimination. The artist, in order to bring out the distinguishing characteristics of his vision of the world, must select and emphasise these features in the real world which illustrate his view. Hardy realised this, and in his private notes he refers to it again and again:

"Art is a changing of the actual proportions and order of things, so as to bring out more forcibly than might otherwise be done that feature in them which appeals most strongly to the idiosyncrasy of the artist."

" ... As, in looking at a carpet, by following one colour a certain pattern is suggested, by following another colour, another: so in life the seer should watch that pattern among general things which his idiosyncrasy moves him to observe and describe that alone. This is, quite accurately, a going to Nature: yet the result is no mere photograph, but purely the product of the writer's own mind."

This is profoundly true and it is true for any artist. It is his capacity to select and isolate what are to him the significant features in the panorama of experience that differentiates the artist from the photographer. But the nature of their vision requires some artists to be much more careful than others to give an illusion of ordinary reality. Jane Austen, for instance, who is out to show us the comedy that lies in the everyday life of the average person, must not allow us to doubt for a moment that we are reading about such a life. We must be under the impression that we are getting a genuine glimpse of an ordinary drawing-room, and listening to the conversations there. Any obvious discrepancy between what she shows us and what we should expect to find in such a drawing-room will destroy this illusion, and with it our belief in her comic vision of life.

Hardy, concerned not with the everyday surface of things but with the deeper principles and forces that lie behind them, does not need to do this. On the contrary, too much preoccupation with the surface of things would distract our attention from the facts which he wishes to emphasise. If our eyes are always being directed to superficial details they will not penetrate below them to perceive fundamental causes: we shall not notice the pattern, to use his phrase, in the carpet of experience which his idiosyncrasy moves him to observe. In consequence, it would be mistaken for him to adopt a realistic convention. As he says, "My Art is to intensify the expression of things so that the heart and inner meaning is made vividly visible," and "Art is a dis-proportioning—(i.e. distorting, throwing out of proportion) —of realities, to show more clearly the features that matter in those realities, which, if merely copied, might possibly be observed, but would more probably be overlooked. Hence 'realism' is not Art." He required a convention that would give full scope for the expression of the spiritual and imaginative aspects of experience, and would eliminate the necessity for describing the mere superficial features of its appearance. Naturally the greater realism, to which the go-ahead novelists of his time were turning, held no attraction for him.

So far from disliking the dramatic intensity and regularity which the first novelists had taken on from the playwrights, he found it necessary for the expression of his vision. He turned backwards, not forwards, in order to discover the most appropriate mode for his art. If he had masters, they are Shakespeare and that British novelist who learnt most from Shakespeare, Sir Walter Scott.

I do not know if you have remarked how often I have mentioned Scott when seeking for a parallel to Hardy. It was inevitable that I should; for Hardy has more in common with Scott than with any other British novelist. Intellectually, of course, they were poles apart. Their kinship is aesthetic. Scott, like Hardy, was inspired by rural life, country humours, traditional customs. His imagination was also fired by ancient stories, ballads and superstitions, and, even more strongly than Hardy, he saw the life of his own day in terms of its history, with every house, every landmark stamped all over by the associations of its past. Further, Scott also envisaged human beings simply and epically— as grand, tragic figures fired by elemental passions. Hardy, therefore, searching for an appropriate form through which to express his inspiration, turned away from his contemporaries—turned away even from George Eliot—to the Waverley novels.

Everything in Hardy's make-up, then—his temperament as well as his circumstances—directed him to adopt the older conventions of fiction. Even in his latest and most experimental book, "Jude the Obscure," he does not escape from it. He may deck it up with realistic trappings, but the substance of Jude's story is old-fashioned tragic drama expressed with old-fashioned tragic eloquence. The rest of Hardy's successful works are conceived firmly within the limits of the older convention. We may sometimes regret this. As I hope to show later on in these lectures, it is responsible for some grave defects in his books. Still, if we are to appreciate him, we must school ourselves to accept these conventions for the time being. It is simply no good going to him expecting the eye-deceiving realism of Tolstoy or the psychological subtleties of Proust. We must read him in the spirit we read "The Antiquary"—or "King Lear," for that matter: prepared to swallow naïve melodramatic plots, full of mystery and coincidence and sensational improbable events, and complete with hero and heroine, villain and comic relief.

III

If we do, we shall not be disappointed. Hardy's talent was equal to its every opportunity. Like his range, it is narrow. He rings the changes on a few situations, a few motives, and a few types of character. He is not a player with many strokes. But those he has are winners.

Within its range Hardy's imagination is unfailingly fresh, unforced, fertile in expression and of the highest power. And it is before all things a creative imagination. If a book is a work of art in so far as the imagination inspiring it has transfigured the author's experience, no novels are more aesthetic than Hardy's. He never presents us with a mere record of his observations; always it is observation coloured by the idiosyncrasy of the artist's personality, vitalised by the energy of the artist's temperament. Hardy's books are always pictures, and never photographs; and we like them as we like pictures—for aesthetic reasons: not only because they recall reality to us but because they stir our emotions directly by their own individual quality.

It is a unique quality too. Hardy may learn from other writers but he never imitates them. His individuality is so strong that it transforms anything he touches. Even when he is bad, it is in his own peculiar way. One paragraph of his sweeps us straight away into the unmistakable atmosphere of Hardy's world.

This imaginative power owes its strange individuality to a mixture of qualities seldom found together. In the first place, it is in the deeper sense in which Hardy uses the word, extremely true to nature. Hardy uses a convention, but it is not an idealising convention. The harsh reality of the world, in which he was brought up, combined with a natural sincerity of disposition to keep him vigilantly faithful to the truth about life as he saw it. Whether he is describing a landscape or a state of mind, he never shuts his eyes to what is ugly in it or what is drab. Indeed, if it were divested of any of its significant qualities, however ugly or drab, the subject would have no interest for him; it would not stimulate his creative powers. To convey the spirit of it as it is, is his sole aim.

On the other hand, the essence which Hardy divines in his subject is not one that would be apparent to an ordinary mind. For the second distinguishing quality about his imagination is that it is poetic. This is such an ambiguous word that you must forgive me if I pause for a moment to explain what I mean by it.

The word poetry is nowadays used habitually in two different senses; it can just mean verse form, as when we say, "I hear Mr. So-and-so writes poetry." But it is also used to denote a certain type of imaginative inspiration, as when we say, "Mr. So-and-so is full of poetic feeling." That is the sense in which I am employing it about Hardy. Now, since this inspiration very frequently expresses itself in verse form, the two have sometimes come to be considered as necessarily connected; and when people find them separate from one another they think there is something wrong. Matthew Arnold meant that there was something wrong in Pope's work when he said he was a classic of our prose. In the same way, people have criticised De Quincey on the ground that although he wrote in prose he was really a poet. Now, of course, this is all nonsense. No subject matter is bound to one form. The fact that most novelists write in prose, and that many lovers choose to express their raptures in verse, does not mean that it is impossible to write a good novel in verse or to make a moving declaration of love in prose. All that matters is that they should be successful.

When I say that Hardy's imagination is poetic, therefore, I mean that it is of a type that more often chooses verse as its mode of expression. In this he is very English. The English literary genius is, most characteristically, a poetic genius. For one good book in prose there are three good English lyrics. The poetic impulse of the English shows itself often in other forms. That drama which is the instrument of England's greatest literary glory is a poetic drama: Shakespeare conceives his picture of life in a mood which requires the lyrical rhythms and heightened imagery of verse for its expression. The novel, too, has been tinged with a poetic spirit. Some of our most famous novelists are poetic in a sense no Continental novelist is. Scott, Dickens, the Brontës, Meredith, D. H. Lawrence, Virginia Woolf present a picture of life intensified by the ardour and freaked by the fancy of a poetic vision. Three of these, moreover (this is noteworthy)—Scott, Emily Brontë and Meredith—are also distinguished poets in verse. Hardy was of the same family. His creative imagination had two strains in it. First, it was intensely poetic; so much so that he thought of himself as a poet rather than a novelist. But there was also in him that love of story-telling, that interest in the lives of human beings that is the characteristic mark of the novelist. And his genius only found complete fulfilment when both these strains in him had scope.

This duality is the central, most important fact about Hardy's work considered in its purely aesthetic aspect. He seems always to have been feeling about for some form which would satisfy both these impulses. He aimed consciously, so his wife tells us, at keeping his narratives at once as close to natural life and as close to poetry as conditions would allow. And he often regretted that conditions would not let him keep them closer still. In his most ambitious work, "The Dynasts," he actually devises a new form to achieve this purpose, combining a realistic study of Napoleonic history, cast in the form of a Shakespearean historical play, with an allegorical drama about personified spiritual forces, modelled on the "Prometheus Unbound" of Shelley. But his novels and poems are also hybrids. Hardy's most characteristic type of poem is a narrative with a contemporary plot, a realistic detailed setting, and told in a colloquial and prosaic diction. This is half-way to a short story. Equally, his novels are half-way to poems. They have a great deal of the normal novel about them—so much so that they could not, most of them, be cast in a verse form. Hardy, like other novelists, wants to give a full-length picture of human life, and he needs the space and flexibility of prose narrative to do this. He could not accumulate the detail necessary to illustrate his drama in the condensed mode of verse. But he did aspire to write a novel which should have the emotional and imaginative intensity of a poem; and those aspects of experience which inspired him to write, and which, in consequence, he wished to emphasise, were those which have more usually stirred writers to choose verse as their vehicle of expression.

"The poet," he once remarked, "takes note of nothing that he cannot feel emotively." In this sense Hardy was a poet in all his work. He is stirred by what is momentous and moving and picturesque in life—by its phases of heightened passion or spiritual illumination; and the picture of the world he desires to present is one in which these hold the centre of the canvas. In consequence, he presents his theme in a higher emotional key than most novelists do, and conceives it in more imaginative terms. Madame Bovary's first meeting with Rodolphe is just as important an event in her life as Bathsheba's first meeting with Troy. It is important in the same way, too. Each woman is encountering the lover who is to bring her to disaster. But in Madame Bovary the encounter is, on the face of it, a perfectly commonplace incident. Rodolphe is calling on Emma's husband on business, and is brought in to be introduced to her as a matter of common politeness. How different is the scene in "Far from the Madding Crowd," when Bathsheba, walking alone through a wood at night, knocks against an unknown man, and then, opening her dark lantern to see who he is, is dazzled by the figure, glittering in scarlet and gold, of the stranger Sergeant. Hetty Sorrel, in "Adam Bede," is arrested for murder, just like Tess; but there is nothing spectacular about the scene of her arrest. In fact, it takes place off-stage. Tess is found by the police, in the first mysterious gleam of dawn, asleep amid the immemorial monoliths of Stonehenge. Hardy seizes every opportunity that his subjects afford for poetic treatment; gets every ounce of picturesque value from that country life which is its subject—from its natural beauty or its historic traditions and association. And, so far as his material has a romantic element in it, Hardy emphasises that romantic element. The life at the dairy where Tess meets Angel, as described by Hardy, is as much an essay in pastoral poetry as an idyll of Theocritus. The military life in "The Trumpet Major" is military life as seen by the poet—steeped in gallant sentiment and brilliant colour, and lilting with martial music. The sordid district of Mixen Lane, in "The Mayor of Casterbridge," where the underworld of the town gathers to plot and revel, is made imaginative by the lurid, macabre light with which Hardy's vision suffuses it. Even when he is out to make an effect of ugliness, he cannot help tinging it with a poetic colour:

"The brown surface of the field went right up towards the sky all round, where it was lost by degrees in the mist that shut out the actual verge and accentuated the solitude. The only marks on the uniformity of the scene were a rick of last year's produce standing in the midst of the arable, the rooks that rose at his approach, and the path athwart the fallow by which he had come, trodden now by he hardly knew whom, though once by many of his own dead family.
'How ugly it is here!' he murmured.
The fresh harrow-lines seemed to stretch like the channellings

in a piece of new corduroy, lending a meanly utilitarian air to
the expanse, taking away its gradations, and depriving it of all
history beyond that of the few recent months, though to every
clod and stone there really attached associations enough and to
spare—echoes of songs from ancient harvest-days, of spoken
words and of sturdy deeds."

This passage illustrates another effect of Hardy's poetic
approach to his subject. He presents the objects of his
description subjectively. He is concerned not only to give
us the facts but to discover their significance to the observer's
imagination. He says somewhere:

"Consider the Wordsworthian dictum (the more perfectly
the natural object is reproduced, the more truly poetic the
picture). This reproduction is achieved by seeing in the heart
of a thing (as rain, wind, for instance), and is realism, in fact,
though through being pursued by means of the imagination it
is confounded with invention, which is pursued by the same
means. It is, in short, reached by what M. Arnold calls 'the
imaginative reason.'"

Hardy's "imaginative reason" is an intensely subjective
affair. His description of anything is soaked in the atmosphere of the mood which it evokes in him, with all the
attendant trains of thought it suggests. Let me give an
example; here are the first paragraphs of "The Woodlanders":

"The rambler who, for old association's sake, should trace
the forsaken coach-road running almost in a meridional line
from Bristol to the south shore of England, would find himself
during the latter half of his journey in the vicinity of some
extensive woodlands, interspersed with apple-orchards. Here
the trees, timber or fruit-bearing as the case may be, make the
wayside hedges ragged by their drip and shade, their lower
limbs stretching in level repose over the road, as though
reclining on the insubstantial air. At one place, on the skirts
of Blackmoor Vale, where the bold brow of High-Stoy Hill is
seen two or three miles ahead, the leaves lie so thick in autumn
as to completely bury the track. The spot is lonely, and when

the days are darkening the many gay charioteers, now perished, who have rolled along the way, the blistered soles that have trodden it, and the tears that have wetted it, return upon the mind of the loiterer.

The physiognomy of a deserted highway expresses solitude to a degree that is not reached by mere dales or downs, and bespeaks a tomb-like stillness more emphatic than that of glades and pools. The contrast of what is with what might be, probably accounts for this. To step, for instance, at the place under notice, from the edge of the plantation into the adjoining thoroughfare, and pause amid its emptiness for a moment, was to exchange by the act of a single stride the simple absence of human companionship for an incubus of the forlorn."

You see how the forlorn loneliness of this autumnal scene is conveyed, partly by descriptive detail—the dripping hedges, the drifts of fallen leaves—but more powerfully by the exactness with which Hardy perceives the melancholy associations which the scene calls up: how he recalls the gay chariots driven by persons now dead that once thronged the solitary road; how he notices that a solitary road is bleaker because more unexpected than the solitary woods that surround it. Such a description is a poet's description. But it is not a novelist's description, according to the practice of most novelists. Turgenev is a writer with a sensibility to natural beauty at least as refined as Hardy's ; and he, too, often begins a story with a picture of its natural setting. But his method is very different. Listen to one of his opening descriptions:

"Give me your hand, reader, and come along with me. It is glorious weather: there is a tender blue in the March sky: the smooth young leaves glisten as though they had been polished. The ground is all covered with that delicate grass with the little reddish stalks that the sheep are so fond of nibbling : to the right and left over the long sloping hillside the green rye is softly waving: the shadows of small clouds glide in thin long streaks over it. In the distance is the dark mass of forests, the glitter of ponds and yellow patches of

D

village: larks are soaring, singing, falling headlong with out-
stretched necks, hopping about the clods. The crows, in the
road, stand still, look at you, pick at the earth. On a hill
beyond a ravine, a peasant is ploughing: a piebald colt with a
cropped tail and ruffled mane is running with unsteady legs
after its mother; its whinnying reaches us. We drive on to
the birch wood, and drink in the strong sweet fresh fragrance."

Is it not a contrast? There is nothing about the spectres
who haunt the road, no whimsical meditation inspired by
the emotion the scene evokes. Turgenev is painter, not
poet. With taste and accuracy he selects the typical features
of the scene and leaves them to rouse the appropriate
emotions in the reader.

Nor is Hardy's poetic method of treatment confined to
description. He tells the story in the same way. Let us
look once again, and more closely, at Bathsheba's first
meeting with Troy:

> "'Is that a dark lantern you have? I fancy so,' said the man.
> 'Yes.'
> 'If you'll allow me, I'll open it and set you free.'
> A hand seized the lantern, the door was opened, the rays
> burst out from their prison, and Bathsheba beheld her posi-
> tion with astonishment. The man to whom she was hooked
> was brilliant in brass and scarlet. He was a soldier. His
> sudden appearance was to darkness what the sound of a
> trumpet is to silence. Gloom, the *genius loci* at all times hither-
> to, was totally overthrown, less by the lantern-light than by
> what the lantern lighted. The contrast of this revelation with
> her anticipations of some sinister figure in sombre garb was
> so great that it had upon her the effect of a fairy transformation."

This scene is vividly presented to the eye, but still more
vividly does Hardy penetrate beneath the material facts to
reveal their imaginative significance. "His sudden appearance was to darkness what the sound of a trumpet is to
silence. . . . The contrast was so great that it had upon her
the effect of a fairy transformation." These sentences are
the operative sentences in the passage, and they are operative

because they drench it in a poetic light. They infuse into the bare facts of the chance encounter that mystery and magic which make it memorable. This mystery and magic spring not from the scene so much as from Hardy's reaction to it, the way in which it sets his fancy working. His creative power shows in his ability to communicate to us, not only the facts of the scene, but its significance to the imagination. It is an extremely good method of description, but not one usually found in a novel. It is the method, not of Flaubert or Tolstoy, but of Keats or Coleridge.

Keats and Coleridge, I need not remind you, were Romantic poets. So was Hardy. The poetic strain in his creative imagination is of the romantic type—sublime, irregular, quaint, mysterious and extravagant, showing itself most typically now in a wild grandeur of conception, now in some vivid particularity of detail. A particular circumstance had accentuated this innate disposition. Hardy started his career as an architect, and the architecture that pleased him best was Gothic church architecture. He thought it the peak of man's artistic achievement. To him, as to all very aesthetically minded spirits, the different arts were of a piece. Further, he noted a special connection between architecture and letters. Both, he said, "were alike, and unlike the other arts in having to convey a rational context in an artistic form." His standard of taste in architecture became his standard of taste in letters. There is nothing classical about it, nothing lucid or symmetrical. It is a Gothic cathedral, all soaring pinnacles and shadowy vistas, clustered over with spreading foliage, and grinning, sinister gargoyles. In addition to being steeped in a poetic mood, his descriptions are thickly embroidered with the freaks of a Gothic fancy:

"It was the first day of June, and the sheep-shearing season culminated, the landscape, even to the leanest pasture, being all health and colour. Every green was young, every pore was open, and every stalk was swollen with racing currents of juice. God was palpably present in the country, and the devil had gone with the world to town. Flossy catkins of the later kinds, fern-sprouts like bishops' croziers, the square-headed moschatel, the odd cuckoo-pint—like an apoplectic saint in a niche of malachite,—snow-white ladies' smocks, the tooth-wort, approximating to human flesh, the enchanter's night-shade, and the black-petaled doleful bells, were among the quainter objects of the vegetable world in and about Weather-bury at this teeming time. . . ."

You can see how Gothic and fanciful this is. Nothing is described plainly and objectively, everything is ornamented in the Elizabethan manner with conceits and similes—the ferns are like bishops' croziers, the cuckoo-pint is like an apoplectic saint, the toothwort like human flesh. They are very odd similes, are they not? Indeed, strangeness is a salient element in Hardy's imagination. Instinctively his eye gravitated towards the queer. He always takes the opportunity to make use of any odd manifestation of Nature's power. Clym makes passionate love to Eustacia out on the heath during an eclipse of the moon, and Hardy emphasises the strangeness added to the scene by the lurid, joyless light in which it is drenched. Even when he is out to give an effect of loveliness and sweetness he likes to blend the strain of oddness with it. May I recall to you the scene when Giles meets Grace home from abroad? He has gone to the market to sell his apple trees, and she catches sight of him standing amid the stone and brick of the town with an apple tree blooming above his head as if it had grown miraculously out of the pavement. We get a pleasant little shock of surprise at the picture of him "standing with his specimen apple tree, the boughs rising above the heads of the farmers and bringing the delightful suggestion of orchards into the heart of the town."

His pictures of the historic past, too, are made vivid by some queer detail. It is instructive to contrast the vision

of the retreat from Moscow in "The Dynasts" with Tolstoy's
in "War and Peace." Tolstoy makes his impression by a
soberly recorded communication of probable facts; we are
told exactly how cold it got, how the French army lost
morale by the gradual increase of discomfort and danger;
all is brought home to us by a thousand details, none particularly striking in itself, but combining to build up an
absolutely solid and convincing picture of despair and
disaster.

Hardy gets his effect in one short scene; and that scene
depends for its force on a single extraordinary, macabre fact.
The pursuing Russians find some French soldiers with their
backs to them, huddling round a fire. These soldiers do not
turn at their approach, and when they get close, they discover
they are stiff; frozen to death in the very act of trying to
get a little warmth into their bodies.

The grotesque is an essential of Hardy's imaginative
make-up. It is a marked characteristic of the plots of his
stories. Here, of course, it can be explained partly in terms
of his philosophy of life. He wants to stress the strange
irony of Fate. Also, as we have seen, he thought that fiction
ought to be odder than life. Did he not model himself on
the Ancient Mariner? But grotesqueness is also a feature
of his taste. Like the Gothic sculptors, he liked gargoyles.
He could convince us that Fate was ironical without making
it play such extraordinary pranks on poor bewildered
mortals. He called one of his collections of short stories
"Life's Little Ironies," and there are moments when he
seems to take a sinister pleasure in presenting Destiny as a
sort of superhuman perpetrator of jokes in poor taste. This
is particularly noticeable in his briefer narratives, "Wessex
Tales," "A Changed Man."[1] What could be more fantastic

[1] This love of sensational plots makes him succeed better in a novel
than in a short story. There is no time in a short story to create the
atmosphere that might persuade us into believing it. We are confronted
with its bones in all their stark improbability.

than the history of the Duchess of Hamptonshire, whose clergyman lover comes back, after years spent in America, to claim his true love, now a widow, only to find that she had travelled, disguised, on the same boat with him, had died during the voyage, and had been consigned to the deep at a funeral conducted by himself!; or that of the Fiddler of the Reels, which recounts how a woman's life is ruined by the fact that when a certain fiddler plays a certain dance-tune, she is constrained to dance and to go on dancing till he stops?

Yet in his greatest work this streak of the grotesque does not dominate his imagination. The other strain in it, the sincere, truthful strain, keeps it in check. For the fantastic is not a necessary stimulant to his creative power. It can work equally vigorously on the normal, given that his subject-matter has sufficient poetic sentiment inherent in it to fire his interest at all. He can extract all the appropriate poetry from the homely gaieties of "Under the Greenwood Tree" — the carol-singers' supper, the wedding breakfast—or from the sober everyday toil of the rural labourer's year, thatching and hedging, reaping and sowing.

Nor does the imaginative atmosphere in which he writes these things diminish their substantial reality. Hardy's world is never dreamlike or phantasmal even when his feet are on the earth. Giles tending the apple trees in the market is a solid flesh-and-blood English working-man, not an idealised Corydon of pastoral poetry. The spring wood in "Far from the Madding Crowd" is a real wood with its ferns and cuckoo-pints and catkins.

Hardy said that the highest art was that which, though changing the appearance of what it describes, only does so in order the better to bring out its essential reality. He himself had this kind of art. In his union of bold fantasy and fundamental truth he is unique amongst English novelists.

To find a parallel we must go back to the anonymous authors of the Border ballads, "Clerk Sanders" and "The Twa Corbies." Like theirs, Hardy's most extravagant flowers of fantasy are firmly rooted in the common soil of human life.

III

HIS ART

I

In my last lecture I sought to define the general character of Hardy's imagination, its blend of hard truth and wild Gothic poetry. In this I want—pursuing my investigation—to trace the mode in which it operates. In what feature of his work does this imagination choose to manifest itself? First of all, in his power of visualisation: his creative power shows itself most continuously and most characteristically in its capacity to embody its inspiration in visible form. Before he does anything else, Hardy wants to make you see with your mind's eye the action of the tale he is telling. Indeed his creative impulse seems to have instinctively expressed itself in picture. He, as it were, begins by drawing the curtain aside and giving you something to look at. Of course, all novelists do this in some degree or other, but many—in particular, those who make their characters real by the accuracy with which they portray their conversation or the workings of their minds—do it only slightly. No other English novelist has so great a power of visualisation: it is Hardy's most important weapon, and it is the basis of his whole method. He constructs his book in a series of scenes. We are always told what we are looking at. His technique, oddly enough, is that of the modern director of films. We watch the story. The scene opens; we take it in with our eyes; then someone begins to speak, and the action gradually unfolds itself. Let me take an example:

> "Along the road walked an old man. He was white-headed
> as a mountain, bowed in the shoulders, and faded in general
> aspect. He wore a glazed hat, an ancient boat-cloak, and
> shoes; his brass buttons bearing an anchor upon their face.

In his hand was a silver-headed walking-stick, which he used as a veritable third leg, perseveringly dotting the ground with its point at every few inches' interval. One would have said that he had been in his day, a naval officer of some sort or other.

Before him stretched the long, laborious road, dry, empty, and white. It was quite open to the heath on each side, and bisected that vast dark surface like the parting-line on a head of black hair, diminishing and bending away on the furthest horizon.

The old man frequently stretched his eyes ahead to gaze over the tract that he had yet to traverse. At length he discerned, a long distance in front of him, a moving spot, which appeared to be a vehicle, and it proved to be going the same way as that in which he himself was journeying. It was the single atom of life that the scene contained, and it only served to render the general loneliness more evident. Its rate of advance was slow, and the old man gained upon it sensibly."

It is only after this, when the road and the old man are clearly before us, that Hardy tells us who he is and what he is doing.

This passage, of course, occurs early in the book, but he continues the same method all the way through. One clear picture succeeds another. When the plot rises to its crisis, Hardy's visualising power burns all the brighter. Once more like a film producer, he often makes his climax a silent one. The dramatic moment expresses itself in action rather than words. Consider that great scene between husband and wife, which is the turning-point in the action of "The Return of the Native." Hardy wishes to indicate that although Clym Yeobright has broken—so he thinks—finally with Eustacia, he is still passionately in love with her:

"She hastily dressed herself, Yeobright moodily walking up and down the room the whole of the time. At last all her things were on. Her little hands quivered so violently as she held them to her chin to fasten her bonnet that she could not tie the strings, and after a few moments she relinquished the attempt. Seeing this he moved forward and said, 'Let me tie them.'

She assented in silence, and lifted her chin. For once at least in her life she was totally oblivious of the charm of her attitude. But he was not, and he turned his eyes aside, that he might not be tempted to softness.

The strings were tied; she turned from him.

'Do you still prefer going away yourself to my leaving you?' he inquired again.

'I do.'

'Very well—let it be. And when you will confess to the man I may pity you.'

She flung her shawl about her and went downstairs leaving him standing in the room."

It is not the dialogue that makes this scene so moving. The dialogue, as a matter of fact, is rather stilted and inexpressive. But the emotion comes through to us; for it is incarnate in every movement and gesture that Clym and Eustacia are represented as making: the quivering of her hands, his involuntary movement forward, the way he turns aside his eyes lest the spectacle of her beauty should compel him to weaken.

Or let us take another scene from "The Trumpet Major," when Bob discovers that John (for all his apparent indifference) really is in love with Anne:

"When supper was over, Bob went outside the house to shut the shutters, which had, as was often the case, been left open some time after lights were kindled within. John still sat at the table when his brother approached the window, though the others had risen and retired. Bob was struck by seeing through the pane how John's face had changed. Throughout the supper-time he had been talking to Anne in the gay tone habitual with him now, which gave greater strangeness to the gloom of his present appearance. He remained in thought for a moment, took a letter from his breast-pocket, opened it, and with a tender smile at his weakness, kissed the writing before restoring it to its place. The letter was one that Anne had written to him at Exonbury. Bob stood perplexed; and then a suspicion crossed his mind that John, from brotherly goodness, might be feigning a satisfaction with recent events

which he did not feel. Bob now made a noise with the
shutters, at which the trumpet major rose and went out, Bob
at once following him."

How many other writers would have tried to express this
in words by some involuntary outburst of speech? It is
typical of Hardy simply to show us Bob silently watching
through the window John's silent caressing gesture.

Hardy achieves the extraordinarily vivid visualisation
mainly in two ways. First of all, his sheer ability to picture
his scene completely. I expect you will remark this in the
description of the old man on the road which I quoted just
now. The broad features are firmly set before us—the road
and the old man. We see him in scale and proportion to the
landscape, which is his setting. This is in the large, heroic,
descriptive manner of Scott. But Hardy does not stop when
he has given us the broad outline, as Scott does. Here he
is more like Richardson. He goes into every detail—the old
man's hat, his buttons and his characteristic sailor's gait—
so that there are no vague, vacant intervals in the picture
which may blur our full impression. The scene is complete.

His second device is more specifically imaginative. He
makes extensive use of arresting similes. There is one in
this passage. The road, says Hardy, bisects the vast dark
surface of the heath "like the parting-line on a head of
black hair." It is a strange simile. But then, Hardy's
Gothic fancy does always run to strangeness, and it is the
strangeness that makes it so vivid. His books are full of
such imagery: the moss-clothed roots of the trees in "The
Woodlanders" looking like "green gloves"; "the bloated
white visage of the winter's day, emerging like a dead-born
child"; the white road running between the sombre Mell-
stock hedges "like a ribbon jagged at the edges." The dark,
stormy waves, edged with foam, that beat against the Cliff
without a Name in "The Pair of Blue Eyes" look like a
funeral pall with a white border. The window-board in

Geoffrey Day's house is stamped with black circles burnt by the heated bottoms of drinking-cups, so that it looks like "an envelope that had passed through innumerable Post Offices." The bloodstain slowly soaking through the floor of the room where Tess has murdered Alec gives the ceiling below the appearance of "a gigantic Ace of Hearts." Of course, by themselves these queer images might merely surprise and disturb, but they rest securely on the accumulation of soberly observed facts with which he builds up his scene, and just colour them with that imaginative light which stamps the scene on our mental eye. By *itself* "the parting on the head of hair" might seem only a conceit; by *themselves* all the facts about the old man on the road would create a picture, solid enough but commonplace. It is the combination of the two which makes it unforgettable.

This method of telling the story in pictures brings with it two advantages. It is by these means that Hardy is able to establish the atmosphere of his world so quickly and so certainly. We do not have to pick it up by hints. We are taken there and shown exactly what it looks like. At once we see how it differs from any other world. Secondly, it helps to keep our interest engaged. First we see the scene, but for a moment we are in suspense as to what is its import. "Who are these people?" we ask ourselves. "Why are they in this place?" Our curiosity is excited and we read on to find out the answer to the riddle. This is the old-fashioned method of telling a tale employed by adventure-story writers, but it is none the worse for that. So many sophisticated artists scorn these simple arts, and, in consequence, their books do not excite our interest easily. We have, as the saying is, to make an effort "to get into them." Hardy, like Shakespeare, does not disdain the tools of the popular writer when composing a serious work of art. As a result, he makes the best of both worlds. We can read his books both in order to get a profound experience and also for the pleasure of losing ourselves in a thrilling tale. Nor are we often bored. Even when the scene is dramatically unimportant our mental eye is entertained.

Moreover, his visualising faculty is sometimes the vehicle of his highest inspiration. Closely associated with his power of visual description is his power of visual invention. It is not just that he makes us see a scene. He invents scenes which, of their very nature, stir the imagination. Not only does he describe the incident graphically; the incident is imaginatively conceived, is in itself mysteriously arresting and exciting. "Far from the Madding Crowd," in particular, is full of such episodes. You may recall that in which Troy, when he is wooing Bathsheba, shows her the regimental sword-drill—how he takes her into a remote fern-filled hollow on the heath and tells her to stand very still. He draws his sword, and in a moment she finds herself "in a whirl of flashing blades that seemed likely every second to pierce her to the heart." It is a vividly imagined scene, but it is more than that. The episode is so strange: the romantic heath, the lonely hollow and the glittering stranger soldier with his dangerous gleaming weapon. And behind this strangeness, and reinforcing it, is the emotion of the drama. For the scene is symbolic. Troy, with his glamour and his ruthlessness, is to be the instrument of Bathsheba's tragedy. He is to take her, as it were, by his sword; in another sense he does pierce her heart with a fatal wound. It is as if Hardy's plot, gathering heat from the passion stored with it, suddenly flamed up in a blaze of poetic invention. Equally evocative is the description of the dying Fanny's last journey through the winter's night to the gate of the Casterbridge workhouse . . . how she drags herself along by telling herself that each milestone in turn is the end of her journey; how, reaching it, she rests a moment and then struggles on till she collapses. Then she catches sight of a passing dog, and, half leaning on it, is pulled to her final destination. The people at the work-house open the door and find her prone on the doorstep. They carry her in, and stone the dog away. The journey through the twilight, huddled on the dog's back, is unforgettable in its strangeness; and how extraordinarily does it convey her complete weakness and destitution! Not a human being is there to pity her; and by the final irony of human fate, that dumb creature who was her only succour is turned with blows from the door. Troy's remorse at her death is conveyed by a similar invention. With a futile gesture of penitence he stays up half the night planting flowers on her grave by the light of a lantern; but when he has gone to bed the storm breaks, and the rain, gushing in a torrent through the mouth of a gargoyle grinning sardonically from the church tower, washes all the plants away. No straight comment by author or actor could so imaginatively express the futility of human repentance in a ruthless universe.

Another triumph in the same kind is the gambling scene in "The Return of the Native." In the hot summer night on the heath, Venn finds Wildeve gambling with Thomasin's precious hoard of guineas on a stone, by the light of a lantern. He sets to work to win them back. Gradually he does so. Wildeve will not stop. Suddenly a moth blunders into the lantern and puts out the light. The heath around trembles with the faint green spark of glow-worms. The players gather a handful together, and, ranging them round the stone, continue their reckless match by the eerie light till Wildeve has lost all. Absorbed in their desperate game, the men forget everything round them. The little noises of the heath go on, and the wild ponies gather with surprised, frightened eyes about them. Once more it is a queer conception; but it is also an intensely dramatic one. Nothing could convey better the obsessed intensity of the passion animating the characters than the contrast between them and the tranquil rural night scene under the open sky, with no human sound—as it would seem—within miles.

Again, what an exquisite invention is that episode in "The Trumpet Major" when Bob, in order to win back Anne, makes her a little Aeolian harp and hangs it at the mill, outside her window, so that the breeze sets its springs a-tremble all through the autumn night, touching her heart to a wistful sadness:

"He arose, and Anne followed with curiosity in her eyes, and with her firm little mouth pouted up to a puzzled shape. On reaching the mossy mill-head she found that he had fixed in the keen damp draught which always prevailed over the wheel an Aeolian harp of large size. At present the strings were partly covered with a cloth. He lifted it, and the wires began to emit a weird harmony which mingled curiously with the plashing of the wheel.

Every night after this, during the mournful gales of autumn, the strange mixed music of water, wind, and strings met her ear, swelling and sinking with an almost supernatural cadence. The character of the instrument was far enough removed from anything she had hitherto seen of Bob's hobbies; so that she marvelled pleasantly at the new depths of poetry this contrivance revealed as existent in that young seaman's nature, and allowed her emotions to flow out yet a little further in the old direction, notwithstanding her late severe resolve to bar them back.

One breezy night, when the mill was kept going into the small hours, and the wind was exactly in the direction of the water-current, the music so mingled with her dreams as to wake her; it seemed to rhythmically set itself to the words, 'Remember me! think of me!'"

Then there is the scene in "The Mayor of Casterbridge," when Henchard wanders on to the bridge of the river, wondering whether he shall kill himself; and then, gazing into the water in the twilight, he sees with a thrill of horror his own drowned body floating pallid on the waves. In reality, it is the effigy of him which his enemies have been parading about the town and have now thrown away. But, for the minute, he takes it as a supernatural omen. The incident conveys his absolute despair, and his sense that he is under a quasi-supernatural curse that he cannot escape. Hardy conveys a similar sense of doom by similar means in "Tess." Do you remember the incident on her honeymoon at the mill, the night after her disastrous confession? She is lying in wakeful misery. Angel, she thinks, is asleep in the next room. He appears, walking in his sleep, picks her up, carries her over the narrow plank that spans the racing mill-stream—how she longs they might both fall and drown together!—and, taking her to the ruined Priory, lays her down in an open stone coffin, and, then, still asleep, picks her up and carries her back once more. The mere conception of the scene has the wild imaginative poetry of Webster; but it also suggests that the superhuman force of Destiny is compelling her irresistibly towards her death, and that Angel is a blind instrument in the hands of this Destiny.

I do not mean to imply that Hardy is anything so crude as an allegorist. Consciously chosen symbols are generally dreadfully unconvincing. Most likely he was hardly aware, when he conceived them, of the deeper implications of these scenes. His creative imagination was on fire, and immediately, instinctively, it embodied itself in these episodes. He just *saw* that the next thing that happened was that Troy showed Bathsheba the sword-drill; or that Angel walked in his sleep and carried Tess to the Priory. The story unfolded itself before him, a passive spectator, as it unfolds itself before us; but, because he conceived his story so imaginatively, its ultimate inspiring sentiment coloured his whole creative process, gave shape to every action and incident that suggested itself to him. This is the gift of the dramatic poet. It is very rare to find it in a novelist. Most novelists with a strain of poetry in their composition express it in the atmosphere which they diffuse round the action of their plot. The sinister atmosphere of the marshes in the beginning of Dickens's "Great Expectations" contributes to the impression the story makes on us. But we could do without it. Though the book would be imaginatively the poorer, the essential drama would remain. Hardy's strain of poetry shows itself not just in atmosphere but in the actual turn of the action, not in the scenery but in the play. These episodes are poetic inventions, the expression of the same concentrated activity of the imagination as a brilliant metaphor or a moving cadence of verse. I do not know where you will find anything like them in fiction, except in "Wuthering Heights." For the best parallel we must leave fiction and go back to the drama, to the Sleep-walking scene in "Macbeth" or the Echo scene in "The Duchess of Malfi."

I must repeat—Hardy's novels are visual novels. It is in his ability to make us "see" that his greatest strength lies. And he relies mainly on it for his effects. If you cut the visual parts out of the novels of Jane Austen, let us say, you would still have the best of them left. If you cut them out of Hardy's, you would not have more than fifteen per cent. The books would be like the performance of an opera with only the libretto and no music. For it is largely by his visualising power that he communicates his vision of experience. His vision of nature, for instance: this is the most characteristic manifestation of his creative power, and it dominates his scene. This was to be expected. For one thing, nature controls the conduct of life in an agricultural community. Hardy, too, as we have seen, always stresses the poetic aspect of his subject-matter. And it is in its connection with nature that the poetry of a countryman's life resides. "That poetry," he says, "which, in spite of the sting of poverty, is inseparable from such a condition of life as the countryman's lies in his absolute dependence on the moods of air, earth and sky. Sun, rain, snow, wind, dawn, darkness, mist, are to him, now as ever, personal assistants and instructors, masters and acquaintances with whom he comes directly into contact, whose varying tempers must be well considered before he can act with effect." Further, nature was to him the emblem of those impersonal forces of Fate with whom he presents mankind as in conflict. In two of his books, "The Woodlanders" and "The Return of the Native," the setting is made to stand for the universe; and in all his other successful works it has symbolic value. Not a background, but an actor in the play, it is always present, the incarnation of a living force with a will and a purpose of its own—now and again taking an actual hand in the story—ruining Henchard's crops, killing Giles—but more often standing aloof, the taciturn and ironic spectator of the ephemeral human insects who struggle on its surface. Always we are aware of nature moving on its appointed course—warming to spring, yellowing to autumn, with recurrent punctuality, careless whether Tess dies or Anne finds her true love. Now and again the personality of nature seems to step forward and with one tremendous gesture dwarf the human beings in the story into insignificance. . . .

"With these words Yeobright went forth from the little dwelling. The pupils of his eyes, fixed steadfastly on blankness, were vaguely lit with an icy shine; his mouth had passed into the phase more or less imaginatively rendered in studies of Oedipus. The strangest deeds were possible to his mood. But they were not possible to his situation. Instead of there being before him the pale face of Eustacia, and a masculine shape unknown, there was only the imperturbable countenance of the heath, which, having defied the cataclysmal onsets of centuries, reduced to insignificance by its seamed and antique features the wildest turmoil of a single man."

Such a passage as this illustrates how Hardy's sense of a fundamental dissonance between man and his environment serves to enrich his work with a special aesthetic effect. We listen, as it were, to two movements, the movement of

man's life and the movement of nature's, counterpointed
one against the other, to produce a complex beauty.

Nature, then, is as important an element in Hardy's vision
of life as it is in one of the regular nature-writers like Wordsworth or Clare; but his view of life makes his vision different
from theirs. There is no Wordsworthian mysticism about
it. He does not represent it as the incarnation of a spirit
"that lives and moves through all things," commanding
man to worship. He did not think there was such a spirit.
The central dogma of his faith was that the universe was a
soulless, automatic process. Further, he would have been
disinclined to worship it even if it had possessed a soul.
For nature, to Hardy, was far from being all beauty and
goodness. It had its beautiful aspects—and no one appreciated them more sensitively—but it had other aspects too:
cruelty, indifference and caprice. Indeed, in nature he saw
repeated the same blind and selfish struggle that he found
in the life of man:

> "They went noiselessly over mats of starry moss, rustled
> through interspersed tracts of leaves, skirted trunks with
> spreading roots whose mossed rinds made them like hands
> wearing green gloves; elbowed old elms and ashes with great
> forks, in which stood pools of water that overflowed on rainy
> days, and ran down their stems in green cascades. On older
> trees still than these huge lobes of fungi grew like lungs. Here,
> as everywhere, the Unfulfilled Intention, which makes life what
> it is, was as obvious as it could be among the depraved crowds
> of a city slum. The leaf was deformed, the curve was crippled,
> the taper was interrupted; the lichen ate the vigour of the
> stalk, and the ivy slowly strangled to death the promising
> sapling."

Here is nothing of that contrast which most writers who
have found inspiration in nature draw between the peaceful,
innocent, natural world and the sin-stained life of man.
"God made the country and man made the town," said
Cowper. Hardy thought that the same force made both,

and that there was nothing divine about its handiwork. Indeed, such manifestations of life as have been touched by the human spirit are superior to those in which nature has its own free way. Man, helpless though he be, can feel pity and sympathy, and can try, even though it be in vain, to deny his own happiness in order to further that of others. Not so nature.

Indeed, the life of nature moves Hardy only in so far as, by similarity or contrast, it illustrates the life of man. Neither he nor his characters ever leave human society to find peace in the contemplation of nature and animals, as Cowper did. His shortest descriptive lyric about nature relates its subject to the life of human beings. "For," said he, "a mark made by man on a scene is worth ten times as much as one made by unconscious nature." He did not even think one could feel attached to a countryside with which one had no human associations:

"But whether he meditated the Muses or the philosophers, the loneliness of Hintock life was beginning to tell upon his impressionable nature. Winter in a solitary house in the country, without society, is tolerable, nay, even enjoyable and delightful, given certain conditions; but these are not the conditions which attach to the life of a professional man who drops down into such a place by mere accident. They were present to the lives of Winterborne, Melbury and Grace; but not to the doctor's. They are old association—an almost exhaustive biographical or historical acquaintance with every object, animate and inanimate, within the observer's horizon. He must know all about those invisible ones of the days gone by, whose feet have traversed the fields which look so grey from his windows; recall whose creaking plough has turned those sods from time to time; whose hands planted the trees that form a crest to the opposite hill; whose horses and hounds have torn through that underwood; what birds affect that particular brake; what bygone domestic dramas of love, jealousy, revenge, or disappointment have been enacted in the cottages, the mansions, the street or on the green. The spot may have beauty, grandeur, salubrity, convenience; but if it lack memories it will ultimately pall upon him who settles there without opportunity of intercourse with his kind."

For Hardy, as for the ancient writers of Greece and Rome, landscape is always a landscape, with figures.

However, this does not diminish the part played by the background in his pictures. On the contrary, it charges it with all the added emotion of the human drama. Hardy's picture of Wessex is the most elaborate study of landscape in English letters. For one thing, it combines, as no other does, breadth and intimacy. Such a writer as Wordsworth confines himself in general to the broad outlines of his subject. Now and again, it is true, he may isolate a detail to make his picture vivid, but he is mainly concerned with its general features. With broad brush he sketches in mountain, lake and sunset sky. A swift dash of yellow indicates a patch of daffodils by the water's edge. They are not painted in detail, and the whole intention of the artist is to draw only so much of the superficial facts of the scene as is needed to indicate to us its general characteristic sentiment. Clare and Cowper, on the other hand, concentrate mainly on the details. With loving, patient accuracy, they put in every small characteristic feature of leaf, bell and stamen.

Hardy combines both methods. Take a characteristic passage, like that which describes Eustacia's lonely vigil on the heath on the night of the 5th November:

"A tract of country unaltered from that sinister condition which made Caesar anxious every year to get clear of its glooms before the autumnal equinox, a kind of landscape and weather which leads travellers from the South to describe our island as Homer's Cimmerian land, was not, on the face of it, friendly to women.

It might reasonably have been supposed that she was listening to the wind, which rose somewhat as the night advanced, and laid hold of the attention. The wind, indeed, seemed made for the scene, as the scene seemed made for the hour.

Part of its tone was quite special; what was heard there could be heard nowhere else. Gusts in innumerable series followed each other from the north-west, and when each one of them raced past the sound of its progress resolved into three. Treble, tenor, and bass notes were to be found therein. The general ricochet of the whole over pits and prominences had the gravest pitch of the chime. Next there could be heard the baritone buzz of a holly tree. Below these in force, above them in pitch, a dwindled voice strove hard at a husky tune, which was the peculiar local sound alluded to. Thinner and less immediately traceable than the other two, it was far more impressive than either. In it lay what may be called the linguistic peculiarity of the heath; and being audible nowhere on earth off a heath, it afforded a shadow of reason for the woman's tenseness, which continued as unbroken as ever.

Throughout the blowing of these plaintive November winds that note bore a great resemblance to the ruins of human song which remain to the throat of fourscore and ten. It was a worn whisper, dry and papery, and it brushed so distinctly across the ear that, by the accustomed, the material minutiae in which it originated could be realized as by touch. It was the united products of infinitesimal vegetable causes, and these were neither stems, leaves, fruit, blades, prickles, lichen, nor moss.

They were the mummied heath-bells of the past summer, originally tender and purple, now washed colourless by Michaelmas rains, and dried to dead skins by October suns. So low was an individual sound from these that a combination of hundreds only just emerged from silence, and the myriads of the whole declivity reached the woman's ear but as a shrivelled and intermittent recitative. Yet scarcely a single accent among the many afloat to-night could have such power to impress a listener with thoughts of its origin. One inwardly saw the infinity of those combined multitudes; and perceived that each of the tiny trumpets was seized on, entered, scoured and emerged from by the wind as thoroughly as if it were as vast as a crater.

'The spirit moved them.' A meaning of the phrase forced itself upon the attention; and an emotional listener's fetichistic mood might have ended in one of more advanced quality. It was not, after all, that the left-hand expanse of old blooms spoke, or the right-hand, or those of the slope in front; but it was the single person of something else speaking through each at once."

This passage reveals an eye for the detail of the country scene only possible to a man who had lived in it from earliest youth. Who else would realise that the wind made a different noise when it was blowing through hollow or heather or over bare stones, let alone be able to distinguish them? And his other senses were as informed as his ear. A page or two later, Hardy discriminates equally precisely the feel to the foot of path, of fern, of heather. "To a walker," he says, "practised in such places, the difference between impact on maiden herbage and on the crippled stalks of a slight footway is perceptible through the thickest boot." Yet this detail is made subordinate to a general picture. We are not shown the heath through a microscope. Clare's eye for small facts is combined with Wordsworth's eye for the general scene. The heath bells are visualised as part of the whole heath, the heath as part of England, and England as part of the earth. Indeed, some of his most memorable descriptions embrace a still greater scope, and reveal their subject in relation to the general cosmic system:

"Norcombe Hill—not far from lonely Toller-Down—was one of the spots which suggest to a passer-by that he is in the presence of a shape approaching the indestructible as nearly as any to be found on earth. It was a featureless convexity of chalk and soil—an ordinary specimen of those smoothly outlined protuberances of the globe which may remain undisturbed on some great day of confusion, when far grander heights and dizzy granite precipices topple down.

The hill was covered on its northern side by an ancient and decaying plantation of beeches, whose upper verge formed a line over the crest, fringing its arched curve against the sky, like a mane. To-night these trees sheltered the southern slope from the keenest blasts, which smote the wood and floundered through it with a sound as of grumbling, or gushed over its crowning boughs in a weakened moan. The dry leaves in the ditch simmered and boiled in the same breezes, a tongue of

air occasionally ferreting out a few, and sending them spinning
across the grass. A group or two of the latest in date amongst
the dead multitude had remained till this very mid-winter time
on the twigs which bore them, and in falling rattled against
the trunks with smart taps.

Between this half-wooded, half-naked hill, and the vague,
still horizon that its summit indistinctly commanded, was a
mysterious sheet of fathomless shade—the sounds from which
suggested that what it concealed bore some reduced resemblance to features here. The thin grasses, more or less coating
the hill, were touched by the wind in breezes of differing
powers, and almost of differing natures—one rubbing the
blades heavily, another raking them piercingly, another brush-
ing them like a soft broom. The instinctive act of human-
kind was to stand and listen, and learn how the trees on the
right and the trees on the left wailed or chaunted to each other
in the regular antiphones of a cathedral choir; how hedges
and other shapes to leeward then caught the note, lowering it
to the tenderest sob; and how the hurrying gust then plunged
into the south, to be heard no more.

The sky was clear—remarkably clear—and the twinkling of
all the stars seemed to be but throbs of one body, timed by
a common pulse. The North Star was directly in the wind's
eye, and since evening the Bear had swung round it outwardly
to the east, till he was now at a right angle with the meridian.
A difference of colour in the stars—oftener read of than seen
in England—was really perceptible here. The sovereign bril-
liancy of Sirius pierced the eye with a steely glitter, the star
called Capella was yellow, Aldebaran and Betelgeux shone
with a fiery red.

To persons standing alone on a hill during a clear midnight
such as this, the roll of the world eastward is almost a palpable
movement. The sensation may be caused by the panoramic
glide of the stars past earthly objects, which is perceptible in
a few minutes of stillness, or by the better outlook upon space
that a hill affords, or by the wind, or by the solitude; but
whatever be its origin, the impression of riding along is vivid
and abiding. The poetry of motion is a phrase much in use,
and to enjoy the epic form of that gratification it is necessary
to stand on a hill at a small hour of the night, and, having first
expanded with a sense of difference from the mass of civilised
mankind, who are dreamwrapt and disregardful of all such pro-

ceedings at this time, long and quietly watch your stately progress through the stars. After such a nocturnal reconnoitre it is hard to get back to earth, and to believe that the consciousness of such majestic speeding is derived from a tiny human frame."

This combination of botanist's microscope and astronomer's telescope is unique, and it gives Hardy's vision of the natural world a unique force. Its detail endows it with the concrete recognisable actuality of something we know. It has also the compelling imaginative power of a picture which exhibits something known in a new, grander perspective, extending our field of vision so that we see what we know in relation to the greater conditioning forces we do not know. Incidentally, the passage is an illustration of how a strong creative imagination can make use of what might seem the most intractable material. The scientific view of the universe, introduced in the Victorian age, is a grim affair. Hardy was only too well aware of this. As we have seen, it made him very depressed. But the poet in him was undefeatable, and, revealed through his eyes, it becomes the opportunity for a new sort of poetry—an awe-inspiring vision of infinite spaces and mysterious, irresistible forces—as compelling to the fancy as any primitive belief in the gods of wind and earth and fire.

Moreover, his vision of landscape embraces yet another dimension. He sees it not only in space but in time. Did you notice how, at the beginning of the passage about Egdon I quoted just now, he remarked that it was unaltered from the time of Caesar? His historic sense makes him perceive, in the scene he is looking at, its connection with the past. Behind its modern actuality stretches the dim vista of its history, peopled by the shadowy figures of its former inhabitants. We are made to see it as part of an eternal process:

"He frequently walked the heath alone, when the past seized upon him with its shadowy hand, and held him there to listen to its tale. His imagination would then people the spot with its ancient inhabitants; forgotten Celtic tribes trod their tracks about him, and he could almost live among them, look in their faces, and see them standing beside the barrows which swelled around, untouched and perfect as at the time of their erection. Those of the dyed barbarians who had chosen the cultivable tracts were, in comparison with those who had left their marks here, as writers on paper beside writers on parchment. Their records had perished long ago by the plough, while the works of these remained. Yet they all had lived and died unconscious of the different fates awaiting their relics."

In a description like this, Hardy recalls yet one more author, Kipling—the Kipling of "Puck of Pook's Hill." No other writer but Hardy has envisaged the English landscape in so many aspects. And, as usual, that mixture of poetry and truth which is the hall-mark of his creative faculty is the chief factor in his achievement. We see Dorset just as it is, with its downs and water-meadows and heath interspersed with strips of oak copse, crowned by beech groves and dimpled with the barrows of the ancient dead: a land of long, gradual slopes and delicate greens and chalky blues and dim browns, stretching beneath the vast wastes of sky, all portrayed, exact and unidealised. Yet the intensity of his imagination enabled him to present it in its sublime relation to space and time, and to vivify it by the infusion of a living spirit; the spirit in which Hardy himself confronted the universe, sad, majestic and enduring.

Hardy recorded nature primarily in its relation to the life of man. Human life, therefore, is an essential feature in his picture of the natural world. His imaginative power shows itself characteristically in his presentation of the rustic scene. He had forerunners here. Though the eighteenth-century novelists did not have much perception of the picturesque qualities of rural life, the Romantic Movement had opened men's eyes to it, and George Eliot and Mrs. Gaskell—to name no others—had decorated their stories with vignettes of country customs and country pleasures. Hardy inherited this tradition of pastoral poetry. The customary rural ceremonies and merry-makings caught his fancy, both from their association with landscape and with the historic past. He always seized the chance to bring one into his stories, and always describes it in detail. The parties in "The Woodlanders" and "Under the Greenwood Tree," with their homely jests and rude plenty and boisterous country dances; winter delights, as when the mummers perform the old Christmas play, "St. George," by the fire-light of Mrs. Yeobright's kitchen, or the carol-singers call Fancy to her window under the frosty starlight; and those of summer—the Maypole, sprung up in the night like Jack's beanstalk, and gay with bluebell and cowslip and ragged robin, which greets Thomasin's eyes when she looks out of her window in the early morning; or the midsummer rites that send the village girls of Hintock stealing through the shadowy woods in the voluptuous June night; the sunburnt Harvest Home supper, with its songs and its cider-drinking, outside Bathsheba's farmhouse,—these are high spots in Hardy's books, and from each he distils its individual perfume of rustic poetry.

Equally sensitively he appreciates the imaginative quality inherent in the ordinary necessary activities of agricultural life: the shepherd's life in "Far from the Madding Crowd"; the furze-cutter's life in "The Return of the Native"; the life of wood and orchard in "The Woodlanders." Do you remember the description of Giles, fresh from cider-making, in "The Woodlanders"?

"He looked and smelt like Autumn's very brother, his face being sunburnt to wheat-colour, his eyes blue as cornflowers, his sleeves and leggings dyed with fruit-stains, his hands clammy with the sweet juice of apples, his hat sprinkled with pips, and everywhere about him that atmosphere of cider which at its first return each season has such an indescribable fascination for those who have been born and bred among the orchards."

Or, still more memorable, the little scene when Marty and Giles plant the trees in the naked January woods?

"What he had forgotten was that there were a thousand young fir trees to be planted in a neighbouring spot which had been cleared by the wood-cutters, and that he had arranged to plant them with his own hands. He had a marvellous power of making trees grow. Although he would seem to shovel in the earth quite carelessly there was a sort of sympathy between himself and the fir, oak, or beech that he was operating on; so that the roots took hold of the soil in a few days. When, on the other hand, any of the journeymen planted, although they seemed to go through an identically similar process, one quarter of the trees would die away during the ensuing August.

Hence Winterborne found delight in the work even when, as at present, he contracted to do it on portions of the woodland in which he had no personal interest. Marty, who turned her hand to anything, was usually the one who performed the part of keeping the trees in a perpendicular position whilst he threw in the mould. . . .

The holes were already dug, and they set to work. Winterborne's fingers were endowed with a gentle conjuror's touch in spreading the roots of each little tree, resulting in a sort of caress under which the delicate fibres all laid themselves out in their proper directions for growth. He put most of these roots towards the south-west; for, he said, in forty years' time, when some great gale is blowing from that quarter, the trees will require the strongest holdfast on that side to stand against it and not fall.

'How they sigh directly we put 'em upright, though while they are lying down they don't sigh at all,' said Marty.

'Do they?' said Giles. 'I've never noticed it.'

She erected one of the young pines into its hold, and held up her finger; the soft musical breathing instantly set it, which was not to cease night or day till the grown tree should be felled—probably long after the two planters had been felled themselves.

'It seemed to me,' the girl continued, 'as if they sigh because they are very sorry to begin life in earnest—just as we be.'"

How incomparably beautiful these passages are! And it is with the characteristic beauty of Hardy's imagination. The scene and the figures in it are not sentimentalised. Giles, in the first passage, is a real working labourer, stained and splashed with pips and apple juice. The process of wood-planting, in the second passage, is detailed to us with sober accuracy. We do not suspect that Hardy has selected only the picturesque aspects of his subject and left the others out. But he responds to the sentiment of the scene so intensely that it infuses the whole picture, making its most prosaic features tremble with beauty. Pastoral poetry can so often provoke a hostile reaction in the reader. Ploughing and sowing may seem picturesque enough to the onlooker, we feel; but to the labourer himself they are only part of his prosaic daily work. It seems as if to represent them poetically were to misrepresent them. We do not feel this with Hardy. On the contrary, only those like Marty, who have planted trees year after year for their daily bread, have achieved that intimacy with such activities which enables them to perceive therein their profounder imaginative significance. Beside Hardy's picture of life, the prettiness of conventional pastoral poetry seems superficial indeed. But equally superficial seems the ugly realism of the author who writes in reaction against it. After all, life on the land has a soul as well as a body. The so-called realist painstakingly describes the body, generally emphasising its more unpleasing features. Hardy pierces beneath these to reveal the soul. To have done this, fully aware of these unpleasing features and unconsoled by any mystical interpretation of the spirit of nature—this is his unique and noble achievement.

II

I have put Hardy's picture of the country and country life first among the manifestations of his imaginative power,

and I have lingered so long over it because it is the most
individual manifestation. No other of our novelists has done
anything like it. But his genius shows itself also in fields
trodden by others. As one expects from a man with so
acute an historic sense, he has got the power to evoke
a past period. This is one of the things in which he shows
his kinship with Scott. His historic imagination embraces
a narrower area, and he gives it rein only in a few short
tales and in "The Trumpet Major." These stories deal
with that same life of rural Wessex that forms the subject
of his other books. Moreover, except in a brief anecdote,
like "The Duke's Reappearance," they take place some
time in the fifty-odd years before his lifetime, more especially the years of the Napoleonic wars. Hardy was right
to limit his historical pictures in this way. It is extremely
difficult to give a convincing account of people in a past
age—that is why there are so few good historical novels.
An imaginative world is real to us because we feel the
people to be living. But the only sort of people we know
intimately enough for us to be able to make a living portrait
of them are the sort of people we have known ourselves.
On the other hand, what strikes us in studying a past age is
the difference between it and our own. It is this difference
we tend to emphasise in any reconstruction of it. This puts
the author of historical novels in a dilemma. Either he must
emphasise the differences between the past and the present,
in which case his characters are generally lifeless puppets,
all helmets and jackboots and mysterious oaths; or, like
Thackeray in "Esmond," he describes his own contemporaries and just puts them into fancy dress, so that we are
conscious of an uncomfortable incongruity between the
characters and their costumes. The successful historical
novelist usually turns out to have chosen a period close
enough to the author's own time for the essentials of human
character not to have changed; but, of course, he must have

a sufficiently acute sense of period to be able to indicate the superficial modifications which differentiate such a period from his own. Hardy realised the problem:

"The house [he remarks in a descriptive passage] was of no marked antiquity, yet of a well-advanced age; older than a stale novelty, but no canonized antique; faded, not hoary; looking at you from the still distinct middle-distance of the early Georgian time, and awakening on that account the instincts of reminiscence more decidedly than the remoter, and far grander, memorials which have to speak from the misty reaches of mediaevalism. The faces, dresses, passions, gratitudes, and revenges of the great-great-grandfathers and grandmothers who had been the first to gaze from those rectangular windows, and had stood under that keystoned doorway, could be divined and measured by homely standards of to-day. It was a house in whose reverberations queer old personal tales were yet audible if properly listened for; and not, as with those of the castle and cloister, silent beyond the possibility of echo."

In his historical reconstructions—the short stories of "The Distracted Preacher" and "The Melancholy Hussar" and the novel of "The Trumpet Major" are the most important instances—he chooses the right period. He was peculiarly well placed, indeed, for writing of the Napoleonic age. When he was a boy, old people still remembered it, and as it had been so sensational an epoch, it had stamped itself with particular vividness on their memories. As a child, he was always hearing stories about it—about the rumours of invasion, the news of Trafalgar, George the Third's visit to Weymouth, the camps of soldiers that established themselves all over the district to withstand possible attack from France. Sometimes he turned one of these anecdotes into a story. There is one about a legend that Napoleon did secretly land by night on the coast, to prospect the ground for invasion and was seen by one of the local inhabitants. "The Melancholy Hussar" tells the tragic tale of a German subject of the

English Crown, come over with his regiment from Hanover, who is hanged for desertion. But "The Trumpet Major" is the chief storehouse of these legends of the past. Hardy says himself that it is more founded on actual hearsay than any other book he ever wrote. Even so, he exhibits his facts in the right perspective for his period. The setting is the Wessex he knew, and the chief characters are humble rustics like those of his acquaintance—the same sort of people as told him the stories, but as they might have appeared in their youth. Only two important historical figures make a personal appearance on the stage, and of these we get no more than a glimpse. George the Third stops to speak to Anne as she walks disconsolately back from seeing the *Victory* go off to sea; Bob Loveday pays a visit to Nelson's friend, Hardy, to ask for a place on his ship. Confined thus to that area of past time which he is in a position genuinely to make living, Hardy performs an amazing feat of historical evocation. The characters are just as real as those in his more contemporary books. We know them equally intimately. Yet he contrives to spread over his whole canvas the colour of the period. So his picture passes the final test of a story set in the past; we can turn from it to an actual record of the time without feeling the slightest change of key.

This power to re-create the characteristic colour of a past age is where his imaginative faculty shows itself. Not only has he chosen the right period—he is also gifted with the right sort of sensibility. Against the unchanging background of sea and downland rises the rural England of Trafalgar, fresh in hue and neat in outline, like one of the coloured prints of the period, with its demure girls in sprigged muslin, its simple, robust enjoyments, its vein of gallant sentiment, its comic country bumpkins, and, leading the procession, the files of England's manly defenders—dashing sailors home from strange lands, laden with parrots and Persian shawls, and spirited soldiers in scarlet coats and white pipe-clayed

breeches, stepping out to the tune of "The Girl I left Behind
Me." The echo of bugle and fife fills the book. Every
incident seems to move in tune with their swaggering martial
rhythm. Like the great historical characters, the great events
are kept off the stage. We get the news of them along with
the other inhabitants of these sequestered villages. Anne
watches the *Victory* as she fades over the horizon on her last
voyage: that is the nearest we get to the Battle of Trafalgar.
But the rumour of Trafalgar, and of the momentous conflict
of which it forms part, hovers always in the background of the
story—now loud, now dwindling almost to inaudibility—but
charging with its own dignity and tension the lives of the
little group of humble persons whose fortunes are the theme
of the story. When Bob is away, he is taking part in an
epoch-making struggle of nations. When John steps out
into darkness, it is to die on some battlefield of Spain.
Finally, once or twice behind the rumour of the great war,
we are made aware of the working of that still vaster historical process in which the war itself is only an episode. A
passing phrase gives us a sense of a remoter past:

> "Thus the troopers crossed the threshold of the mill-house,
> and up the passage, the paving of which was worn into a
> gutter by the ebb and flow of feet which had been going on
> there ever since Tudor times."

Or, casting a glance into the future, Hardy makes us realise
that the laughing, striving handful of human beings who
move so vividly before us are also transient, and in a few
years will be as much a portion of that irretrievably vanished
past as the former inhabitants of their dwellings:

> "At twelve o'clock the review was over, and the King and
> his family left the hill. The troops then cleared off the field,
> the spectators followed, and by one o'clock the downs were
> again bare. They still spread their grassy surface to the sun
> as on that beautiful morning not, historically speaking, so very
> long ago; but the King and his fifteen thousand armed men.

the horses, the bands of music, the princesses, the cream-coloured teams—the gorgeous centre-piece, in short, to which the downs were but the mere mount or margin—how entirely have they all passed and gone!—lying scattered about the world as military and other dust, some at Talavera, Albuera, Salamanca, Vittoria, Toulouse, and Waterloo; some in home churchyards; and a few small handfuls in royal vaults."

Or again:

"The present writer, to whom this party has been described times out of number by members of the Loveday family and other aged people now passed away, can never enter the old living-room of Overcombe Mill without beholding the genial scene through the mists of the seventy or eighty years that intervene between then and now. First and brightest to the eye are the dozen candles, scattered about regardless of expense, and kept well snuffed by the miller, who walks round the room at intervals of five minutes, snuffers in hand, and nips each wick with great precision, and with something of an executioner's grim look upon his face as he closes the snuffers upon the neck of the candle. Next to the candle-light show the red and blue coats and white breeches of the soldiers—nearly twenty of them in all besides the ponderous Derriman—the head of the latter, and, indeed, the heads of all who are standing up, being in dangerous proximity to the black beams of the ceiling. There is not one among them who would attach any meaning to 'Vittoria' or gather from the syllables 'Waterloo' the remotest idea of his own glory or death."

Hardy extends our field of vision to embrace this larger vista very rarely; but always with enormous effect. Once more his method is like that of the maker of moving pictures. We see the period in close-up; and then, for a brief moment, the camera is moved backwards, and it is revealed in its place in the long perspective of time past and time to come. Somehow this makes it more real to us. We are looking at the past from the solid known standpoint of our own age. We hold the threads, that bind us to it, in our hands; and this convinces us of its actuality. And the vision has the pathos that comes from Hardy's intense sense of the frailty, the ignorance of human beings. Sitting in Overcombe Mill, laughing and drinking in the pride of their youth, the soldiers do not know the fate in store for them. . . . "There is not one among them who would gather from the syllables 'Waterloo' the remotest idea of his own glory or death." The trifling scene at the Mill becomes a window through which we are suddenly vouchsafed a glimpse of the sad, mysterious fleetingness of human existence.

III

Hardy's creative power also shows itself in his characters. Indeed, he would not have been a great novelist if it had not. For a novel is a story about human beings, and if we are not made to feel they are convincing human beings their story does not move us. Hardy's stories do move us. Not, indeed, that his characters dominate his books as those of Dickens' do, for instance. The nature of his creative range prevented this, as I sought to show in an earlier lecture. If man is presented to the reader as the helpless creature of impersonal circumstances, the circumstances become as important as the man. He certainly cannot dominate them. Further, we also saw that Hardy is concerned with man rather than with individual men. The differences between John and Henry are not so important in his portrait as the qualities they share. Indeed, quite apart from the limitations imposed by his range, Hardy did not have the power to conceive character very variously. Here his talent is a narrow one compared with that of some writers. His memorable characters all have a family likeness. Most of them, indeed, can be grouped into a few simple categories. There is the staunch, selfless, tender-hearted hero—Gabriel Oak, Giles Winterborne, John Loveday, Diggory Venn; there is the dashing,

fickle breaker of hearts—Troy, Wildeve, Fitzpiers, d'Urberville; there is the patient, devoted, forgiving woman—Tess,
Marty, Elizabeth-Jane; there is the wilful, capricious, but
fundamentally good-hearted girl—Bathsheba, Grace, Fancy,
Anne; there is the passion-tormented, romantic enchantress
—Eustacia, Mrs. Charmond, Lucetta, Lady Constantine.
To these basic types he added a group conceived in a
more intellectual vein. Angel and Knight are doctrinaires;
sensitive men who come to grief through an inability to
realise that human beings are not what their theories have
taught them they should be. Sometimes he modifies one
type by mixing in a quality from another. There is a streak
of Eustacia's passionate splendour in Bathsheba; Bob Loveday, though a warm-hearted, sympathetic character, has a
touch of Troy and Wildeve's fickle shallowness. We feel
the family likeness somehow, even in those figures who
cannot be placed in the categories. Henchard and Clym,
Jude, Mrs. Yeobright are composed of the same elements,
ruled by the same passions as their companions, though
these elements and passions may be mixed in different proportions. And when Hardy deliberately attempts to break
away into a new type he fails in the end to make it intrinsic-
ally different from the old. Sue, in "Jude," is intended to
be a portrait of the advanced woman of Hardy's day—
neurotic and intellectual. Painstakingly he makes her talk at
length about the marriage problem and the difficulties of
religious belief; but her conversation does not ring true—
it is not the expression of her personality. The basic structure of her character is conceived on the old lines. Under
her Ibsenite skin Sue is the sister of Grace and Anne and
Bathsheba.

Hardy's view of life made this kinship between his
creatures inevitable. Always he conceives man in relation
to ultimate human destiny, and in such a relation only
certain qualities strike him as significant. In a harsh world

he sees man as thirsting for happiness and imagining that he will find it by love in some form or another. This love may make him selfless or selfish, forgiving or resentful; he may struggle or he may submit; but his object is always the same, and he reacts to circumstance in one of these ways. In "Jude," as a matter of fact, he attempts something different. Jude, as originally conceived, is actuated by the desire for knowledge as well as the desire for happy love. But before a third of the book is over, the desire for knowledge is forgotten and love becomes Jude's ruling motive, as it was Henchard's and Giles's and Gabriel's.

Such are the elements which compose Hardy's picture of human nature; such are the groups into which his characters divide themselves. He does not succeed in drawing these types equally well. Here, once more, we come up against the limitations of his creative range. Brought up in a peasant community, he can only successfully vitalise characters of a peasant-like simplicity. This cuts out the Knight–Angel type. To draw the self-conscious intellectual needs a deeper acquaintance with sophisticated human nature than Hardy possessed. Again, Hardy's range does not include great ladies. In consequence, Lady Constantine and Mrs. Charmond are not very memorable characters. It is a question of presentation as well as conception. Hardy's characters are made living to us by their conversation. We recognise them because we get to know their voices and tricks of speech. The only mode of speech which Hardy can vividly reproduce to us is that of the Wessex countrymen. Angel and Mrs. Charmond, Knight and Lady Constantine converse in a stilted, impersonal fashion. "Am I to believe this?" cries Angel at the climax of his tragedy. "From your manner I must take it as true; you cannot be out of your mind . . . my wife, my Tess, nothing in you warrants such a supposition as that." This is as lacking in individuality as a conversation translated from a foreign language. Now listen

to the breathing, burning, human eloquence of Henchard
at a crisis in his fortunes:

> "'Don't ye distress yourself on my account. I would not
> wish it—at such a time, too, as this. I have done wrong in
> coming to 'ee—I see my error. But it is only for once, so for-
> give it. I'll never trouble 'ee again, Elizabeth-Jane—no, not
> to my dying day! Good-night. Good-bye!'"

How the flavour of his personality and the vibration of his
passion show themselves in the turn of each phrase, the
cadence of each rhythm!

It was particularly important, moreover, for Hardy that
he should be able to convey his characters' manner of speech,
for by the convention of fiction-writing he had chosen—the
old-fashioned convention of the school of Fielding—it is
largely by means of dialogue that the characters reveal themselves. It would not matter so much to an author employing
another convention. Henry James, for instance, makes all
his people talk in exactly the same way, a way—it may be
incidentally observed—in which no one in heaven or earth
ever talked except Henry James himself. But his characters
are not lacking in vitality, for they live less through their
talk than through their creator's insight into the workings
of their mind and conscience. Hardy, however, exhibits his
characters first by their actions, secondly by their words.
Their inner life is left to our imagination, so that if their
speech does not reveal their individuality, we never get to
know it. Indeed, Hardy's genius made his method of drawing character even simpler and more summary than that of
the school from which he learned his art. For, concentrated
as he is exclusively on the grand tragic issues of human fate,
his characters live in virtue of their vitality when such issues
are in question. The actions he emphasises are momentous
actions that reveal their fundamental motives and feelings—
like Clym's involuntary shrinking from meeting Eustacia's
eyes when he is tying her bonnet. The characteristic

significant speeches for which we remember them are those they utter at the crises of their fortunes. Was he not a poetic dramatist among novel-writers, intent always on charging his stories with the intensity of poetry? It is when his plots call for such intensity that his creative imagination really gets to work on the characters. They live for us in so far as their creator makes living the poetic aspect of their personalities.

This means another limit to his range. He can only draw at full length people whose nature is of sufficiently fine quality to make them realise the greatness of the issues with which they are involved. It is no good looking to him for a vivid portrait of a trivial or superficial person. His imagination passes them by. For Hardy to bring a character to life, it must be of a temperament to feel passionately and profoundly; it must be aware of itself as a victim of human fate; otherwise, he cannot enter into it. And it must have that magnetism or beauty of nature which makes a poetic presentation appropriate. Hardy could not have drawn Mrs. Bennett, for Mrs. Bennett was aware of no more important problem than that of marrying her daughters to rich husbands, while a picture of her suffused with poetry would not have been a picture of Mrs. Bennett at all. We may note also in this connection that Hardy is seldom successful at drawing odious people. Odiousness implies meanness; and mean people neither feel deeply nor are aware of any issues larger than those involved in the gratification of their selfish desires. If Hardy does try to draw such persons, it is a dreadful failure. Alec d'Urberville is just the conventional vile seducer of melodrama. Hardy cannot get inside such a person and see how life looked to him. Not that his successful creations are all virtuous—Henchard and Eustacia, to name no others, commit sins in the grand manner. But it *is* the grand manner, the expression of an overmastering passion, not the calculated consequence of selfish lust. Moreover, they know they are wrong—they are torn with conscience. We do not dislike them. We are not meant to. "Eustacia was, in some ways, lovable," says Hardy.

Hardy's range of character, then, is limited. But when he chooses a subject fully within these limitations, when he is drawing a native of the Wessex country with deep feelings and susceptible of finer issues, he is superbly successful; the peculiar composition of his imaginative faculty turns into an asset. Once more, as in his picture of nature, truth and fancy reinforce each other. The figures are made of solid flesh and blood: they are not the least sentimentalised or inflated. Giles and Fancy, Gabriel and Bathsheba, are recognisable human English people, who can eat and drink and take their clothes off, and be irritable and foolish and excited just like you and me. Yet their figures are touched with an imaginative light to glow forth with a special pathos, an added majesty. Hardy can make us realise certain aspects of them which we should have noticed if we had known them, but which are very hard to convey in a book. Romantic charm, for instance: he is one of the few novelists who can make us appreciate why the heroes are in love with the heroines. What wax dolls most heroines of English fiction are, especially the gentle, passive ones! Think of the heroines of Scott and Dickens. Many of Hardy's are just the same type: Thomasin, for instance, in "The Return of the Native," is tender and faithful and timid, just like a heroine in the Waverley novels. But they are insipid; and she is not. His poetic faculty enables him to suffuse her personality with the innocent, romantic grace which was her attraction. His visual faculty helped him here. He can give the charm of a woman's appearance:

"A fair, sweet, and honest country face was revealed, repos-
ing in a nest of wavy chestnut hair. It was between pretty
and beautiful. Though her eyes were closed, one could easily

imagine the light necessarily shining in them as the culmination of the luminous workmanship around. The groundwork of the face was hopefulness; but over it now lay like a foreign substance a film of anxiety and grief. The grief had been there so shortly as to have abstracted nothing of the bloom, and had as yet but given a dignity to what it might eventually undermine. The scarlet of her lips had not had time to abate, and just now it appeared still more intense by the absence of the neighbouring and more transient colour of her cheek. The lips frequently parted, with a murmur of words. She seemed to belong rightly to a madrigal—to require viewing through rhythm and harmony."

Thomasin is a living figure to us from the way that such a passage as this conveys her characteristic attraction. We know her, not through any special insight into her character, but through our realisation of the individual minor-key sweetness of her personality. Hardy's sensibility to feminine charm and his power to discriminate its distinguishing quality is the chief means by which he makes his heroines live: whether it be Fancy's wilful, innocent coquetry, or Bathsheba's ardent glowing smiles and tears, or Anne's demure rural neatness, or Eustacia's sombre gorgeousness:

"She was in person full-limbed and somewhat heavy; without ruddiness, as without pallor: and soft to the touch as a cloud. To see her hair was to fancy that a whole winter did not contain darkness enough to form its shadow; it closed over her forehead like nightfall extinguishing the western glow.

Her nerves extended into these tresses, and her temper could always be softened by stroking them down. When her hair was brushed she would instantly sink into stillness and look like the Sphinx. If, in passing under one of the Egdon banks, any of its thick skeins were caught, as they sometimes were, by a prickly tuft of the large *Ulex Europaeus*—which will act as a sort of hairbrush—she would go back a few steps, and pass against it a second time.

She had Pagan eyes, full of nocturnal mysteries, and their light, as it came and went, and came again, was partially hampered by their oppressive lids and lashes; and of these the under lid was much fuller than it usually is with English

women. This enabled her to indulge in reverie without seem-
ing to do so: she might have been believed capable of sleeping
without closing them up. Assuming that the souls of men and
women were visible essence, you could fancy the colour of
Eustacia's soul to be flame-like."

The peculiar charm of each character exhales from her every
movement like the perfume from a flower. These women
stamp themselves most on our memories in those heightened
moments when their fascination, putting forward its full
power, compels the hearts of men. Bathsheba caught looking
at herself bewitchingly in the looking-glass as she rides on
top of the farm cart to her new home; Eustacia watching
the embers of the bonfire in the November darkness of the
heath, in these episodes Hardy crystallises the particular
qualities in the personality which gives it its magic. We see
them from the lover's angle: they are real in so far as their
romantic aspect is real. It is only one aspect. But since
Hardy's stories are love stories, it is enough to make them
convincing for his purpose.

The same strain in his imaginative genius enables him to
convey beauty of character. He excels at drawing good
people. Here again he is unusual. Many writers fail over
good characters, because they cannot take goodness naturally. Concerned primarily to give a convincing picture of
average mankind, they are flummoxed by the task of describing outstanding virtue. Their hand falters, they take their
eyes off their object—which is life—and begin to copy some
lifeless model of ideal goodness. Further, the goodness
which will move the reader must have a gleam of heaven in
it—some finer nobility, some intimation of the ideal. Most
novelists are too earthbound, too "prose-minded," to be
able to communicate this. In their efforts to do so, they
cease to make their characters living. Hardy's genius enables
him to avoid these pitfalls. He can easily convey the gleam
of heaven, just as he can convey the romance exhaling from

his heroines: and he is not the least flummoxed by the spectacle of outstanding virtue. His simple, ardent, epic eye envisaged life as an affair of high lights and strong qualities. Mankind, to him, always assumed the heroic proportions of a figure seen against the vast sky of Destiny; and its virtues assumed heroic proportions too. He can make Gabriel and Marty and Giles convincing portraits of English rustics, and yet imbue them with the fidelity that no defeat can shake, the courage that will face catastrophe unmoved, the "charity that hopeth all things and endureth all things." The beauty of their natures is as unselfconscious and inevitable as that of a tree or a flower.

A single-minded intensity of nature is needed to fire his talent. Single-mindedness is the one quality which is common to all Hardy's successful studies of character. Grand, passionate and simple are the themes which inspired him; grand, passionate and simple are the characters in which his creative power shines brightest. They vary, as we have seen. Marty and Giles and Tess are simply faithful; Mrs. Yeobright is grimly obsessed; Henchard and Eustacia possessed by passion. But in each the pulse of life beats higher than in the ordinary person. They feel more strongly, reflect more profoundly. The eyes of each are fixed upon one object, for which they are prepared to sacrifice anything; and if they fail to get it, their life is ruined. Hardy's talent is such that he can incarnate this intensity of temperament convincingly in a human being. Once more a solid sense of earthy reality unites with imaginative force to achieve a new creation.

There is one category among Hardy's characters which I have not mentioned—what may be called Hardy's "chorus" characters, the groups of rustics which in his greatest works form, as it were, the chorus to the main drama: the choir led by tranter Dewey in "Under the Greenwood Tree"; the turf-cutters in "The Return of the Native"—Fairway,

Christian, Grandfer Cantle and the rest; the cottagers of
Little Hintock—Wood, Cawtree, Upjohn, Crendon; the
Casterbridge gossips in "The Mayor of Casterbridge";
Bathsheba's labourers in "Far from the Madding Crowd"—
Joseph Poorgrass, Henry Fray, Billy Smallbury, Jan Coggan;
the grave-diggers in "A Pair of Blue Eyes"; Haymoss,
Blore and the rest of Lady Constantine's tenantry in "Two
on a Tower." They cannot be compared with the central
figures in the drama just because they are placed in the story
to provide a chorus. They always appear in a group, never
separately. They are not full-length portraits. Moreover,
they are drawn in a different convention. Here Hardy is in
the straight tradition from Shakespeare. These minor characters are the direct descendants of Bottom and Dogberry
and the rustics who gather in response to Falstaff's call to
arms at the house of Justice Shallow—"character parts,"
as they say on the stage, made up of a few strongly marked,
deliberately caricatured personal idiosyncrasies. They need
not fear comparison with their ancestors. Rich fragments of
rusticity, they are as entertaining as any of the classic comic
characters of Fielding or Goldsmith. But, unlike theirs and
like Shakespeare's, they can also stir serious emotion.

"'And she was as white as marble-stone,' said Mrs. Cuxsom.
'And likewise such a thoughtful woman, too—ah, poor soul—
that 'a minded every little thing that wanted tending. "Yes,"
says she, "when I'm gone, and my last breath's blowed, look
in the top drawer o' the chest in the back room by the window,
and you'll find all my coffin clothes; a piece of flannel—that's
to put under me; and my new stockings for my feet—they are
folded alongside, and all my other things. And there's four
ounce pennies, the heaviest I could find, a-tied up in bits of
linen, for weights—two for my right eye and two for my left,"
she said. "And when you've used 'em, and my eyes don't
open no more, bury the pennies, good souls, and don't ye go
spending 'em, for I shouldn't like it. And open the windows
as soon as I am carried out, and make it as cheerful as you can
for Elizabeth-Jane."'

'Ah, poor heart!'

'Well, and Martha did it, and buried the ounce pennies in the garden. But if ye'll believe words, that man, Christopher Coney, went and dug 'em up, and spent 'em at the Three Mariners. "Faith," he said, "why should death rob life o' fourpence? Death's not of such good report that we should respect 'en to that extent," says he!'

'"Twas a cannibal deed!' deprecated her listeners.

'Gad, then, I won't quite ha'e it,' said Solomon Longways. 'I say it to-day, and 'tis a Sunday morning, and I wouldn't speak wrongfully for a zilver zixpence at such a time. I don't see noo harm in it. To respect the dead is sound doxology; and I wouldn't sell skellintons—leastwise respectable skellintons— to be varnished for 'natomies, except I were out o' work. But money is scarce, and throats get dry. Why *should* death rob life o' fourpence? I say there was no treason in it.'

'Well, poor soul; she's helpless to hinder that or anything now,' answered Mother Cuxsom. 'And all her shining keys will be took from her, and her cupboards opened; and little things 'a didn't wish seen anybody will see; and her wishes and ways will all be as nothing!'"

This has the same pathos and eloquence as Dame Quickly's account of Falstaff's death. And, like Shakespeare, Hardy evinces the poet's power of universalising the particular. The passage has a significance transcending the situation it describes. "Why should death rob life o' fourpence?" There is a timeless proverbial quality about the homespun phrase. We forget Solomon Longways and seem to be listening to the voice of all humble humanity as, from the wisdom of its hard workaday experience, it makes un-illusioned its comment on the mystery of death.

Indeed, these characters—it is their most important function—are necessary to set Hardy's main and serious drama in perspective with human life as a whole. The chorus is the symbol of the great majority of humdrum mortals, who go on living through their uneventful day, whatever catastrophes may overtake the finer spirits placed among them. Henchard and Eustacia may love and suffer and die; but the rustics go on. It is they who bring the children to birth, dance at the wedding, mourn at the grave-yard, and speak the epitaph over the tomb. They are eternal as the earth by which they live. And their very prosaicness anchors the story to reality. It gives the reader a standard of normality by which he can gauge the tremendous heights and depths to which the main characters rise and fall. In his last two big novels, "Tess" and "Jude," he leaves them out. And they lose by it. We feel them to give a distorted picture of life, as his greatest works do not. Nor, for all that they are drawn in so stylised a convention, are these figures unreal. Taken individually, they may seem ex-aggerated, but taken—as they are meant to be taken—in a corporate mass, they build up a picture of average mankind in its rural manifestation that is carved out of the bedrock of life.

This chorus provides also the chief occasion for Hardy's humour. Humour is not the quality that one might expect to find in him, so grand and so gloomy as he is. But it is there all right. Nor is it incongruous with the rest of his achievement. It is rustic, it is elemental, it is grotesque, it is Gothic, it is traditional. Like the characters who are its subject, it descends directly from Shakespeare and the Elizabethans. Here, again, it differentiates his picture of the rural scene from that of the George Eliot school. In the first place, it is not satirical. Hardy does not make us laugh by the brilliant penetration with which he exposes his characters' foibles and follies. His are the jokes and anecdotes that enliven the evenings in cottage and village inn, and, like theirs, his primary aim is simply to make us laugh. The mood which inspires them is simple, genial enjoyment—the countryman's slow relish of the absurd for its own sake. The main themes are the themes of most country humours—the naïve credulity of yokels and of crusted old eccentrics. We are made to laugh at the im-memorial butts of village life—garrulous, reminiscent old

grandfathers, henpecked husbands, ludicrous, timid simple-
tons, and the incongruity between the facts of life and the
countryman's ignorant comment on them. Hardy's mode
of conveying this humour is also Elizabethan. It is leisurely
—there is nothing sharp or slick about it—and it is adorned
with a flourish of whimsical fancy. Now and again there is
a touch of the grave-diggers in "Hamlet" about it—of the
Elizabethan taste for the macabre. Hardy's sense of the
irony of human destiny enables him to get a good deal of
hearty fun out of coffins and funerals:

> "'Ah, poor Lord George!' he continued, looking contem-
> platively at the huge coffin; 'he and I were as bitter enemies
> once as any could be when one is a lord and t'other only a
> mortal man. Poor fellow! He'd clap his hand upon my
> shoulder and cuss me as familiar and neighbourly as if he'd
> been a common chap. Ay, 'a cussed me up hill and 'a cussed
> me down; and then 'a would rave out again, and the goold
> clamps of his fine new teeth would glisten in the sun like
> fetters of brass, while I, being a small man and poor, was fain
> to say nothing at all. Such a strappen fine gentleman as he
> was too! Yes, I rather liked 'en sometimes. But once now
> and then, when I looked at his towering height, I'd think in
> my inside, "What a weight you'll be, my lord, for our arms to
> lower under the aisle of Endelstow Church some day!"'"

The quotation illustrates another quality of Hardy's
humour—perhaps its most distinctive quality. It is verbal
humour, dependent for its effect upon the particular words
he uses. That poetic strain which was intrinsic to his
imaginative process gives him a delight in speech, so that his
humour has a literary quality denied to more sophisticated
humour.

> "'Happy times! heavenly times! Such lovely drunks as I
> used to have at that house! You can mind, Jacob? You used
> to go wi' me sometimes.'
> 'I can—I can,' said Jacob. 'That one, too, that we had at
> Buck's Head on a White Monday was a pretty tipple.'
> "'Twas. But for a wet of the better class, that brought you

no nearer to the horned man than you were afore you begun, there was none like those in Farmer Everdene's kitchen. Not a single damn allowed; no, not a bare poor one, even at the most cheerful moment when all were blindest, though the good old word of sin thrown in here and there at such times is a great relief to a merry soul.'

'True,' said the maltster. 'Nater requires her swearing at the regular times, or she's not herself; and unholy exclamations is a necessity of life.'"

*   *   *   *   *

"'But this deceiving of folks is nothing unusual in matrimony,' said Farmer Cawtree. 'I know'd a man and wife—faith, I don't mind owning, as there's no strangers here, that the pair were my own relations—they'd be at it that hot one hour that you'd hear the poker, and the tongs, and the bellows, and the warming-pan, flee across the house with the movements of their vengeance; and the next hour you'd hear 'em singing "The Spotted Cow" together, as peaceable as two holy twins; yes—and very good voices they had, and would strike in like street ballet-singers to one another's support in the high notes.'

'And I knowed a woman, and the husband o' her went away for four-and-twenty year,' said the bark-ripper. 'And one night he came home when she was sitting by the fire, and thereupon he sat down himself on the other side of the chimney-corner. "Well," says she, "have ye got any news?" "Don't know as I have," says he; "have you?" "No," says she, "except that my daughter by the husband that succeeded 'ee was married last month, which was a year after I was made a widow by him." "Oh! Anything else?" he says. "No," says she. And there they sat, one on each side of that chimney-corner, and were found by the neighbours sound asleep in their chairs, not having known what to talk about at all.'"

*   *   *   *   *

"'And if Jim had lived, I should have had a clever brother! To-morrow is poor Jim's birthday. He'd ha' been twenty-six if he'd lived till to-morrow.'

'You always seem very sorry for Jim,' said old William musingly.

'Ah! I do. Such a stay to mother as he'd always ha' been! She'd never have had to work in her old age if he had continued strong, poor Jim!'

'What was his age when 'a died?'

'Four hours and twenty minutes, poor Jim. 'A was born as might be, at night; and 'a didn't last as might be till morning. No, 'a didn't last. Mother called 'en Jim on the day that would ha' been his christening day if he had lived; and she's always thinking about 'en. You see, he died so very young.'

'Well, 'twas rather youthful,' said Michael.

'Now to my mind that woman is very romantical on the matter o' children?' said the tranter, his eye sweeping his audience."

"Unholy exclamations"; "romantical on the matter o' children"; "flee across the house with the movements of their vengeance,"—do you notice how verbal the humour is? how dependent on its phrasing for its effect? And do you remark its fanciful quality? Humour of this kind is as much an expression of the creative spirit as poetry. To make a joke of something means, by definition, to alter it, not just to leave it as it is. It is not odd that so imaginative a talent as Hardy's should be humorous.

Finally, his creative faculty shows itself in a more general aspect of his work—what I must vaguely call the atmosphere and tone with which he chooses to envelop each particular story. Many novelists have conceived a book originally in terms of a character. "I thought of Mr. Pickwick," said Dickens when asked what had been the original inspiration of "The Pickwick Papers." With other writers—Henry James, for instance—the original germ has been a situation out of which the completed story gradually grew. Hardy's books seem rather to have come into his mind in pictorial terms; as a design in a certain style, harmonised by a prevailing unity of tone. He calls "Under the Greenwood Tree" an essay in the Dutch school of painting. He wanted to give an impression of the rustic life of his youth, and he conceived it as a series of pictures painted with the delicate exactness of detail and the mellow colouring of Vermeer or Hobbema. No violent event is permitted to disturb the desired atmosphere of rural peace. "The Trumpet Major" is an essay in the same kind, but here the impression is modified by a difference in the subject-matter. The scene is not just rural life. It is rural life during the Napoleonic wars. In consequence, it is drawn on a different scale. Seen against that historic background, the figures look smaller and the emotional tone is deepened by the wistful sadness at the brevity of things human which is stirred by the contemplation of a former age.

The love stories of "Two on a Tower" and "A Pair of Blue Eyes" are drawn in sharper outline, coloured in a higher key—pure, ethereal and lyrical—in which the background is less human, more imaginative. The tense elemental pathos of Elfride's drama finds expression in the elemental surging of the Atlantic Ocean on whose shore she dwells. Lady Constantine's single-minded, obsessing passion shows up starkly against the starry vastness of the night sky as seen from the astronomical observatory where she and her lover have their secret meetings. The bleak tragedies of Jude and Tess and Henchard have a similar simple unity of tone; but it is a sterner, harsher simplicity, not lyrical but epic. These books are like gigantic sculptures carved in granite. "Far from the Madding Crowd" is more brilliant in colouring. Here the full-blooded joys and sorrows of the rural scene compose a picture of a glowing Titian-like type, mingling rich shadow and golden sunshine. Darkness, stormy darkness, relieved at moments by a flash of lightning and stirred by the rush of the wind, is the pervading note of "The Return of the Native." Most of its great scenes take place at night, and even day is made dusky by the black stretches of Egdon Heath which is the theatre of its drama. "In Egdon," says Hardy, "night falls earlier than other places." The sad, beautiful tale of "The Woodlanders" is a harmony in quiet half-tones and pale glancing lights. Steeped in a mood of pensive autumnal reverie, the dawn breaks, the trees drip, heavy with moisture, and all draws to a close in misty moonlight.

It is a beautiful close; and this, too, is characteristic of Hardy. For books conceived in this aesthetic way, the end and the beginning are very important. If the author wants his story to move in a particular key, he must strike the keynote right away. Hardy has an extraordinary genius for striking this keynote. In the first paragraph the mood of the book is decisively established. He contrives to do this by various devices. Sometimes he begins with a scene. The curtain rises on "The Mayor of Casterbridge" to reveal a country road stretching away into the distance, and the weary figures of Henchard and his wife and child trudging along it. This road is an image of the bleak pilgrimage which is to be the subject of the story. The opening of "Jude" shows us poor little Jude saying farewell to the schoolmaster who has given him that first glimpse of the finer life of the mind which he is to pursue so vainly in his mature life. The contrast between what Jude is born to and what his nature aspires to, on which the drama hinges, is stated in the first chapter.

"Under the Greenwood Tree" is both a picture of country life and scenery and a study of the old sort of village choir. Accordingly, Hardy introduces us straight away to the choir gathered together. But they are not in church. They are going carol-singing on a winter's night under the greenwood tree. The two themes of the story are combined.

In others of his books—"The Trumpet Major," "A Pair of Blue Eyes," "Far from the Madding Crowd"—Hardy strikes his keynote by a different device: he describes a person. We are shown the face of one of the leading characters in close-up; then, when we are acquainted with it, the camera moves back so that its vision now reveals the setting in which the character is standing.

"The Woodlanders" and "The Return of the Native"

employ yet another method. In both these books the scene largely determines the action. The drama arises from the fact that the characters are confined together in Egdon Heath or in the woods of Hintock. To bring this out, he presents us first of all with a picture of the landscape. It is only when this is firmly established in our minds that he directs our gaze to the chief characters.

I quoted the opening paragraphs of "The Woodlanders" in an earlier lecture. In "The Return of the Native" he essays a similar effect on a grander scale. It is the most tremendously conceived of all Hardy's openings. In four pages of sustained eloquence he conveys to us an impression of the black, inhospitable moorland stretching as far as eye can reach beneath the gathering winter twilight: the harsh heath, unaltered in the memory of the human race. It is only when its solemn spirit has sunk deep into our consciousness that the sound of the human voice is allowed to interrupt this silence. And that silence is felt all through the book—an ironical comment on the cries and protests of the handful of ephemeral human beings who for a brief space disturb its monotony.

Hardy's ends are as memorable as his openings. In the last paragraph he strikes the keynote again, and in so doing makes clear the trend of the action which has preceded it. Sometimes he points a moral. Let me quote the last words of "The Mayor of Casterbridge":

"Her teaching had a reflex action upon herself, insomuch that she thought she could perceive no great personal difference between being respected in the nether parts of Casterbridge, and glorified at the uppermost end of the social world. Her position was, indeed, to a marked degree one that, in the common phrase, afforded much to be thankful for. That she was not demonstratively thankful was no fault of hers. Her experience had been of a kind to teach her, rightly or wrongly, that the doubtful honour of a brief transit through a sorry world hardly called for effusiveness, even when the path was suddenly irradiated at some half-way point by daybeams rich as hers. But her strong sense that neither she nor any human being deserved less than was given, did not blind her to the fact that there were others receiving less who had deserved much more. And in being forced to class herself among the fortunate, she did not cease to wonder at the persistence of the unforeseen, when the one to whom such unbroken tranquillity had been accorded in the adult stage was she whose youth had seemed to teach that happiness was but the occasional episode in a general drama of pain."

These stern sentences do not seem at first glance to refer immediately to the drama which has preceded them; that drama is the tragedy of Henchard, and his fate was too disastrous adequately to be met even in this mood of sober resignation. But they have a deeper and more significant connection with his story, for they relate it to the general experience of mankind. This is what we must all feel, says Hardy, about a world in which such a fate as Henchard's is possible, even if we have been fortunate enough to escape it. Suddenly we see the particular instance in its place in the universal scheme.

He ends "Tess" also with a generalisation. "Justice was done," so the last paragraph begins, "and the President of the Immortals . . . had ended his sport with Tess." But here Hardy has been too deeply moved by Tess's agony to detach himself from it in the same way. The words are a defiant, despairing cry against the injustice of the universal plan.

Hardy's books do not always end thus on a crashing major chord. He is also master of the dying fall, the Miltonic close in calm of mind, all passion spent, the fading echoing music that, when soft voices die, vibrates in the memory. "Under the Greenwood Tree" presents us with an example. It has a happy ending. All is well. The worthy hero is married to the charming heroine, and amid the cheers of their neighbours they drive off to their own home.

The risk about such an end is that it may seem too sweet

and sunshiny. Hardy with a single stroke avoids this. Although Fancy, the heroine, is genuinely in love with her husband, she had hesitated to accept him: for Mr. Maybold the clergyman had proposed to her and, tempted by the position of clergyman's wife, she had almost to the last meditated marrying him instead. She has never dared to admit this weakness to her lover:

> "Amid a medley of laughter, old shoes, and elder-wine, Dick and his bride took their departure, side by side in the excellent new spring-cart which the young tranter now possessed. The moon was just over the full, rendering any light from lamps or their own beauties quite unnecessary to the pair. They drove slowly along Yalbury Bottom, where the road passed between two copses. Dick was talking to his companion.
> 'Fancy,' he said, 'why we are so happy is because there is such full confidence between us. Ever since that time you confessed to that little flirtation with Shiner by the river (which was really no flirtation at all), I have thought how artless and good you must be to tell me o' such a trifling thing, and to be so frightened about it as you were. It has won me to tell you my every deed and word since then. We'll have no secrets from each other, darling, will we ever?—no secret at all.'
> 'None from to-day,' said Fancy. 'Hark! what's that?'
> From a neighbouring thicket was suddenly heard to issue in a loud, musical, and liquid voice:
> 'Tippiwit! swe-e-t! ki-ki-ki! Come hither, come hither, come hither!'
> 'O, 'tis the nightingale,' murmured she; and thought of a secret she would never tell."

This does not strike a jarring note; but there is a gentle irony about it. Even the best wives, so Hardy hints with a tender smile, keep secrets from their husbands. Thus he disinfects our memory of the book from the taint of over-sweetness.

More beautiful, because more poignant, is the close of "The Trumpet Major." John Loveday has unselfishly recognised that Anne loves his brother more than himself,

and, concealing his broken heart under a smile, he goes off
to the war:

"The candle, held by his father, shed its wavering light on
John's face and uniform, as, with a farewell smile, he turned
on the doorstone, backed by the black night; and in another
moment he had plunged into the darkness, the ring of his smart
step dying away upon the bridge as he joined his companions-
in-arms, and went away to blow his trumpet till silenced for
ever upon one of the bloody battlefields of Spain."

These quiet sentences at once bring out the pathetic
tragedy of John's fruitless love, and also indicate that greater
background of the wars of nations which is so essential an
element in the general conception of the story. John may
have loved in homely Dorset, but he is to die on the battlefields of Spain; while the mere mention of his bugle sets
the passage trembling into a music that we bear in our hearts
long after it is heard no more.

Even this passage must give place, however, to that which
closes "The Woodlanders." Grace is walking home with
her husband past the graveyard where Giles lies buried; at
the grave itself stands Marty, the poor girl who had loved
him in vain but who, unlike Grace, was faithful to him
after death:

"Immediately they had dropped down the hill she entered
the churchyard, going to a secluded corner behind the bushes,
where rose the unadorned stone that marked the last bed of
Giles Winterborne. As this solitary and silent girl stood there
in the moonlight, a straight slim figure, clothed in a plaitless
gown, the contours of womanhood so undeveloped as to be
scarcely perceptible in her, the marks of poverty and toil
effaced by the misty hour, she touched sublimity at points,
and looked almost like a being who had rejected with indifference the attribute of sex for the loftier quality of abstract
humanism. She stooped down and cleared away the withered
flowers that Grace and herself had laid there the previous
week and put her fresh ones in their place.

'Now, my own, own love,' she whispered, 'you are mine,

and only mine; for she has forgot 'ee at last, although for her you died! But I—whenever I get up I'll think of 'ee, and whenever I lie down I'll think of 'ee again. Whenever I plant the young larches I'll think that none can plant as you planted; and whenever I split a gad, and whenever I turn the cider wring, I'll say none could do it like you. If ever I forget your name let me forget home and heaven! ... But no, no, my love, I never can forget 'ee; for you was a good man, and did good things!'"

IV

Humour, character, landscape, vividly depicted scenes, tales brilliantly opened and eloquently ended,—it is by means of these that Hardy's imagination casts its spell upon us. But behind them all, heating his apprehension of them to an extraordinary intensity, lies something else—an unusual emotional force. His books communicate a much higher temperature of feeling than most novels do. This feeling is simple in quality, as we should expect. It is no use going to Hardy for subtle sentiments or complex states of emotion. All the same, his emotional range is not narrow in the sense that his range of character is; for it embraces both the heights and the depths of the emotional scale, from black despair to ecstatic joy. There is, unexpectedly, a great deal of joy. Hardy's pessimism did not spring from a low-spirited temperament. On the contrary, the same sensibility that made him so acutely susceptible to life's sorrows made him also exquisitely responsive to its joys.

"Sweet cyder is a great thing,"

he sings in one of his lyrics,

"A great thing to me,
Spinning down to Weymouth town
By Ridgway thirstily,
And maid and mistress summoning
Who tend the hostelry:
O cyder is a great thing,
A great thing to me!

The dance it is a great thing,
    A great thing to me,
With candles lit and partners fit
    For night-long revelry;
And going home when day-dawning
    Peeps pale upon the lea:
O dancing is a great thing,
    A great thing to me!

Love is, yea, a great thing,
    A great thing to me,
When, having drawn across the lawn
    In darkness silently,
A figure flits like one a-wing
    Out from the nearest tree:
O love is, yes, a great thing,
    A great thing to me!

Will these be always great things,
    Great things to me? . . .
Let it befall that One will call,
    'Soul, I have need of thee':
What then? Joy-jaunts, impassioned flings,
    Love, and its ecstasy,
Will always have been great things,
    Great things to me!"

I must ask you to linger on this poem for a moment, even though I am supposed to be lecturing on his novels. For into it is distilled the very essence of this phase of his temperament. It is a poem about pleasure, straightforward, light-hearted, orthodox pleasure, such as the average person looks for in his moments of relaxation. Its theme is drinking and dancing and light love. Writers on the grand scale, like Hardy, seldom have much feeling for this sort of pleasure; the taste for pleasure implies a streak of animal gaiety which is seldom an ingredient in the composition of majestic personalities. But Hardy had it—pessimistic, mournful Hardy! When the normal people round him let themselves go at a party, he did not instinctively stand aside, aloof and unresponsive. On the contrary, he was infected by their spirit—he wanted to join in. From the time he was a boy and used to go fiddling with his father, he loved parties. But his enjoyment was enhanced by the finer strain in him; he saw the party imaginatively, it was lit with the light of poetry. The consequence is that no other of our novelists has described parties so enchantingly: the feast in "Far from the Madding Crowd"; the wild, riotous gaiety round the bonfire in "The Return of the Native"; the Christmas evening with the mummers, and the dance at tranter Dewey's inn in "Under the Greenwood Tree." Hardy's descriptions of dancing are especially memorable—he loved it himself as a young man. To the end of his life the names of the old dance-tunes—"The Lady's Triumph," "The Dashing White Sergeant"—struck a wistful, responsive chord in his heart. They were not the languid, unsociable peregrinations of the modern dance, but the old country dances, festive, communal and energetic, all leaps and twirls and linked hands. They went on and on, until the chalk rose in clouds from the floor and the sweat shone on the dancers' foreheads. Hardy felt the sheer joy in rhythmic animal activity which was part of the pleasure they gave; but he responded also to the more delicate sentiment which blended with it—the lilting sweetness of the music, and, trembling through all, the vibration of romantic sexual feeling. The dance is gay, but it is passionate also.

"Eustacia floated round and round on Wildeve's arm, her face rapt and statuesque; her soul had passed away from and forgotten her features, which were left empty and quiescent, as they always are when feeling goes beyond their register. How near she was to Wildeve! it was terrible to think of. She could feel his breathing, and he, of course, could feel hers. How badly she had treated him! yet, here they were treading one measure. The enchantment of the dance surprised her. A clear line of difference divided like a tangible fence her experience within this maze of motion from her experience without it. Her beginning to dance had been like a change of atmosphere; outside, she had been steeped in arctic frigidity by comparison with the tropical sensations here. She had entered the dance from the troubled hours of her late life as one might enter a brilliant chamber after a night walk in a wood."

Equally well does Hardy communicate the quality of a dreamier, more elegiac pleasure. Do you remember the scene in "The Mayor of Casterbridge" when Farfrae, on his first evening in the town, sings the songs of his country to the handful of rustics who are gathered in the bar of the "Three Mariners," so that their eyes fill with unbidden tears? Or Fancy's walk in the twilight with Dick; or Tess stealing at sunset through the untended patch of wilderness to listen to Angel playing his harp in solitude? In these incidents Hardy evokes those chance moments—we have all experienced them—when ordinary existence is suddenly flooded with an emotion, strange, beautiful, unforgettable, and the sense of life—poised for a fleeting instant between ecstasy and tears—seems almost too poignant to bear. Poignant because it is frustrated. We are made aware of a capacity for bliss in ourselves not to be satisfied in the wearisome condition of mortality.

On the other hand, Hardy's emotional force enables him to convey with equal and terrible impressiveness how little blissful reality can be. He expresses pain more often than pleasure, and all sorts of pain, from Bathsheba's tired wistful sadness as, seated in the churchyard in the dusk, she listened to the choirboys' singing and felt that she "would have given anything in the world to be as those children were," to Eustacia's surging agony on the night of her death as she roams wildly over Egdon, or the eerie terror that breathes from Susan's dark cottage room, gleaming in the firelight, as with unholy rites she sets Eustacia's waxen effigy to waste in the flame—there is a whiff of "Macbeth" in this scene;

from Tess's dull anguish as she labours in the January winds on the Flintcombe farm, to the catastrophic final despair of Henchard.

I have said that love is the dominating motive in Hardy's stories—love conceived as a blind, irresistible storm. It is by means of his emotional intensity, that he is able to bring home to us its power. No one describes love more impressively than Hardy. But he does not analyse its workings like Proust, or show how it manifests itself differently in different characters like Jane Austen. He is concerned less with lovers than with love, less with the effect that passion has on human beings than with its intrinsic quality. He wishes to make us feel the actual heat and colour of its flame, to reproduce its impact on the heart. It is the approach of the lyric poet, of Burns, of Shelley. Hardy's picture of love is in the lyrical manner. Exquisitely he sounds the different notes in its scale—the peaceful, idyllic love of Fancy and Dick; the faithful, enduring, unhopeful love of Gabriel and Marty; Eustacia's searing passion.

Finally, it is his emotional force which makes him able to rise to the heights of tragic feeling required to do justice to his tragic themes. This is why he is most convincing in scenes of death or catastrophe, why his characters live most vividly at the grand and desperate crises of their fortunes. Far from such moments putting a strain on his creative faculty, it is only then that it rouses itself to full activity. Compare his portrait of Eustacia with George Eliot's Maggie Tulliver: both are passionate women whose passions involve them in tragedy. Maggie is an extraordinarily clearly realised personality during that major part of her story when nothing violently sensational is happening to her. But when her whole world falls in pieces round her and she dies in the flood, she loses individuality and becomes a conventional, melodramatic figure. George Eliot's imagination does not work on this plane—she has to fall back on convention.

Eustacia is just the opposite of Maggie. She seems a trifle
stilted in ordinary life: could any old sea-captain's daughter
seem such a tragedy queen all the time? we ask ourselves.
But when the storm breaks on her, when she in her turn has
to despair and drown, how her creator's imagination rises
to realise every vibration of her feelings. Hardy's great
characters are all greatest in their most tragic moments:
Tess, forsaken by Angel; Marty, keeping her lonely vigil
over Giles's grave; Clym, gazing down at the dead wife who
can never now hear his words of forgiveness; Mrs. Yeobright, dying, she thinks, repudiated by her only son, alone
on the heath beneath the pitiless August sun; above all,
Henchard, sinking to death in complete despair in the ruined
cottage on Egdon. Do you remember the will that he leaves,
pencilled on a crumpled scrap of paper?

> "That Elizabeth-Jane Farfrae be not told of my death, or
> made to grieve on account of me.
>
> & that I be not bury'd in consecrated ground.
> & that no sexton be asked to toll the bell.
> & that nobody is wished to see my dead body.
> & that no murners walk behind me at my funeral.
> & that no flours be planted on my grave.
> & that no man remember me.
> To this I put my name.
>
>   'MICHAEL HENCHARD'."

Realistic truth and imaginative power here unite Hardy to
achieve their most tremendous effect. The plain words are
perfectly in character, just what an uneducated farmer like
Henchard might write. But Hardy has managed to charge
them with all the emotional grandeur of great tragedy. He
has achieved his purpose of giving a novel the imaginative
force of poetry—and the highest poetry, the poetry of the
book of Job.

The effect of this intensity is all the greater for the breadth
of his emotional range. If Hardy was always tragic, we

should not be so moved. The reader ceases to respond if he is always required to do so in the same way. But Hardy at his best does not weary us with one emotional note. Our feelings, refreshed by a moment of beauty, can melt into tears easily enough when sorrow seeks to evoke them. And besides, it is because we know that Hardy can feel joy and gaiety that his tragedy strikes us with such terrible conviction; because we know that to the end of his life, he felt cider and the dance and love to be great things for him, that we listen—sadly aware that he may possibly be right—when in another mood he sings:

> "Close up the casement, draw the blind,
>   Shut out that stealing moon,
> She wears too much the guise she wore
>   Before our lutes were strewn
> With years-deep dust, and names we read
>   On a white stone were hewn.
>
> Step not forth on the dew-dashed lawn
>   To view the Lady's Chair,
> Immense Orion's glittering form,
>   The Less and Greater Bear:
> Stay in; to such sights we were drawn
>   When faded ones were fair.
>
> Brush not the bough for midnight scents
>   That come forth lingeringly,
> And wake the same sweet sentiments
>   They breathed to you and me
> When living seemed a laugh, and love
>   All it was said to be.
>
> Within the common lamp-lit room
>   Prison my eyes and thought;
> Let dingy details crudely loom,
>   Mechanic speech be wrought:
> Too fragrant was Life's early bloom,
>   Too tart the fruit it brought!"

HIS WEAKNESS

THE Athenians, it is said, grew weary of hearing Aristides called "The Just." And you may, I fear, have grown weary of hearing me call Hardy a creative genius. If so, the following pages may bring you relief; in them I propose to examine Hardy's faults. For he was a faulty writer—so faulty that, in spite of all his gifts, his most successful works are stained by noticeable blemishes, and his least successful are among the worst books that ever came from the pen of a great writer. His genius works in flashes. When the flash comes it is dazzling, but out it goes, and then the reader is left in the dark, groping about, bothered and bewildered. Like Dickens or Scott, Hardy is liable at any moment to let us down. The reason for this is that his equipment for the task was as defective on one side as it was rich on another. The creative gift, the power to apprehend his material aesthetically, he possessed in the highest degree; but, for complete success, a writer cannot rely on the aesthetic qualities alone. He must know how to present his imaginative conceptions to best advantage. For this he needs the critical qualities—the qualities of craft. Hardy was a great artist, but not a great craftsman.

This appears, first of all, in the design of his books. A craftsman's gift shows primarily in his ability to construct a fitting form in which to incarnate his inspiration. Hardy took trouble to do this: and indeed there are many worse designers. His plots are clear; and he sticks to them. All the same, his hold on design is slack and clumsy. In "Two on a Tower," for instance, form and content have no organic connection. The story describes the romance of Lady Constantine and the young astronomer, St. Cleeve, and the germ of the conception, the idea that inspires Hardy to write it, is the contrast between the cold inhuman stellar universe, which is the theatre of the hero's professional activities, and the hot human passions agitating the two chief characters. It is an imaginative idea, most effectively symbolic of that conflict between man and the nature of things which is a root inspiration of Hardy's creative process. But, in order to make a full-length novel about it, Hardy incorporates it in an intricate and improbable tale of intrigue in high life, featuring a jealous peer and an unscrupulous bishop, and interspersed with reflections on the difficulty of woman's lot in conventional society. This plot is feeble in itself, and it has nothing to do with the imaginative stimulus which prompted him to write the book. The two pull against each other. The more we are moved by the spectacle of the love scenes under the stars, the more are we annoyed when we are forced to divert our eyes from it in order to follow the working of the plot. Indeed, even if he had thought of a better story, Hardy would not have got over his difficulty, for his germ idea, imaginative though it be, is not suitable to a novel. It is not capable of sufficiently varied development. The poetic strain in Hardy's creative process here led him astray. This limited his choice of themes in a way that more prosaic talents are not limited. The theme had to be of a kind susceptible to poetic treatment, and yet it must be full enough to fill a novel. Such themes exist. The emotions stirred by "The Woodlanders" or "The Return of the Native" are of lyrical force; yet they demand a story long and complex enough to make a novel. In fact, you could not have explored all their imaginative possibilities in a short poem. This is not so with "Two on a Tower." The contrast between the stellar universe and human passion is too simple a theme. For the stellar universe is uninhabited and cannot be made to produce the variety of subject and character needed to develop the drama to novel length. Once the author has realised the feelings of Swithin and

Lady Constantine, and related them to their background, he has exhausted the artistic potentialities of his subject. Lack of critical sense has led Hardy to choose fiction as the vehicle for an inspiration which is appropriate only to a lyric.[1] He falls into the same error in "The Well-Beloved." This tells how a man fell in love with a mother, a daughter and a granddaughter, for instinctively he is drawn to the mysterious quality constant in one family. This theme could, of course, have been developed to novel length if Hardy had approached it in a spirit of psychological interest. But he was not a psychologist. It is just the idea of a family face, with its own mysterious, unique fascination, appearing generation after generation, which fires his fancy. Looked at in this way, the theme affords enough material for a ballad, not for a novel; and, in fact, "The Well-Beloved" has to be eked out with an irrelevant and conventional plot. Perhaps he could have made a short novel in verse out of it—something like Patmore's "Angel in the House." It is interesting that Patmore—a very acute critic—did urge him on one occasion to put his novels into verse form. And in this instance he would have been right. Hardy's lack of critical sense leads him to misunderstand the nature of his inspiration, and therefore to choose the wrong mode for its expression.

These books, though, are among Hardy's failures. At his best, he does choose themes for which fiction is the right form. Even then, however, he often executes his design loosely and carelessly. Consider the last part of "The Woodlanders." Clearly, after Giles's death, the trend of the story makes it inevitable that Grace should be reconciled with Fitzpiers. In fact, it is so obviously the logical conclusion of the story that it should be got done with as quickly as is decently possible: Hardy takes forty pages over it!

[1] He did write two lyrics inspired by this theme : " At a lunar eclipse " and " In vision I roamed " ; and has no difficulty in concentrating the whole fertilising content of " Two on a Tower " into their brief span.

H

The reader grows impatient to reach a goal so long in sight, and his impatience brings with it a most undesirable slackening of emotional tension. A similar disproportion also mars "The Trumpet Major." Here Hardy's primary intention is to give us a series of pictures of Wessex life during the Napoleonic period, and he threads these pictures together on the string of a love story—the love story of Anne and the two Loveday brothers. It is a sufficiently adequate string for the purpose, but Hardy does not stretch it taut enough. In order to make room for all his pictures, he ekes out the plot by repeating the same incidents in slightly varied form several times; first, Anne is shown as preferring Bob, then John, then Bob, then John, then Bob again. No development of character is revealed by these fluctuations in her feelings. They are the consequence of outside events, arbitrarily introduced by Hardy to make the story long enough. The result is that the book, delightful though its separate episodes may be, is a little monotonous as a whole.

The novel is peculiarly liable to expose an author's weakness in the art of design. For it sets him some peculiarly difficult problems. The novel proposes to give a convincing picture of real life; but, like other works of art, it is only successful if it composes its material in an orderly pattern. Life, however, fecund, heterogeneous life, is anything but orderly. How then is he to satisfy both his obligations? How is he to devise a picture which satisfies us equally as a pattern and as an illusion of life? How is he to reconcile form with fact? It can be done, even by authors working within as strict a convention of plot as Hardy did. Jane Austen, to name no others, did it. Her stories are exquisitely shapely, and yet create a convincing illusion of reality. Not so Hardy. His vision of life is effective enough. Even though it is not a realistic one, it has the profusion and energy of reality. But, in order to force it into a pattern, he tends to impose a plot on it which is not convincing at all. There is an instance of this at the crisis of "The Woodlanders." In order to achieve the reconciliation between Grace and Fitzpiers, Hardy has to get rid of Mrs. Charmond, who has been seducing Fitzpiers's truant heart away from Grace. It should not have been beyond the mind of man to invent some probable way of doing this. Fickle, and capricious as she is, she might have tired of Fitzpiers; she might even have contracted an illness and died, without putting too great a strain on our credulity. Hardy, however, scorns such unsensational devices; and instead invents a desperate foreign lover for her, who arrives at the hotel where she is staying abroad and shoots her. Hardy does not even describe the lover in detail. He has made a brief appearance once or twice in the story before—not enough for us to get to know his personality. The actual murder is hurriedly reported, second-hand. The lover is revealed as what he is—a piece of machinery, introduced in order to give form to the plot. In "A Laodicean," again, Abner Power has to be got out of England in order that his niece shall marry the hero. It seems that there is no special reason why he should go; so Hardy suddenly tells us that, in his earlier days, he had been an international spy, and that someone had found this out and has now taken to blackmailing him, so that he has to flee the country. The incident is unlikely in itself, it jars violently with the prevailing tone of the story—a social comedy—and there is nothing in Power's character, as described up till then, to make one expect it of him. But the most disastrous example of Hardy's failure in this kind is in "Tess of the d'Urbervilles." It is essential to the development of his plot that Alec should get Tess into his clutches again after she has been deserted by Angel. But how is this going to be managed? For Tess had never liked Alec and now hated him as the author of all her woes. Indeed, he has been presented to us—in so far as he has any individuality at all—as a cigar-smoking, rich young vulgarian, living only for his own animal pleasure. Hardy, however, suddenly reintroduces him into the book in the unexpected character of a Revivalist preacher. Alec, he tells us, has been converted. Far be it from me to deny that pleasure-loving vulgarians can undergo religious conversions. But the event is too odd for the reader to be expected to accept it without explanation. Alec should have been described to us as possessing some emotional streak in his disposition which might make such an occurrence probable. Hardy never attempts to do this: indeed, when, once more for the purposes of the plot, Alec has to behave like a villain again, Hardy simply says airily that his conversion lost its power and that he has reverted to what he was before. All through his books, the reader is liable to knock up against these crude pieces of machinery, tearing the delicate fabric of imaginative illusion in tatters.

The novelist has not finished his task when he has reconciled form with fact. His second problem is to reconcile fact with imagination. He has to give a convincing impression of the real world, but he has also to express his personal vision. And he only achieves complete success in his art if he satisfies both these conditions equally. This is an even harder problem. Many distinguished novelists have never achieved it. "Women in Love" blazes with the fire of Lawrence's temperament. But as a picture of county society in twentieth-century England it is—to say the least of it—far-fetched. Gissing, on the other hand, gives us a most reliable record of the life of the serious-minded poor in Victorian London. But it is only intermittently tinged with an individual colour. Hardy is no more successful than these eminent authors. He errs, as we might expect, with Lawrence rather than with Gissing. His creative power is so much stronger than his critical sense that he always disregards probability if it stands in the way of the emotional impression he wishes to make. As a matter of fact, he was not a good judge of probability. The plot of "The Return of the Native" in the form we possess it concludes with the marriage of Venn and Thomasin. But Hardy did not originally intend to end it like this. He had conceived Venn as a sort of benevolent, mysterious spirit, who appears, from no one knows where, to save Thomasin at the crises of her fortunes, and then, once more, vanishes into obscurity. This, however, would have meant that the book ended sadly for everyone concerned in it. Not only Clym and Eustacia, but the virtuous Venn and Thomasin would fail to attain happiness. His publishers told Hardy that the public would not stand for this; and in deference to his publishers Hardy modified his plan. He regretted doing so, because a happy end conflicted with the aesthetic image he had formed of Venn. But the publisher was right, if the claims of probability were to be respected. Venn did want to marry Thomasin. Once she was free, he would certainly have asked her, and Thomasin—a clinging, timid woman, left alone when still young—would almost certainly have accepted a lover so attractive and who had treated her so nobly. Hardy does not seem to have considered this. If an idea pleased his imagination, that was good enough for him.

Alas! Hardy did not always have the luck to be saved from himself in this way. We see this in two of his most famous books—"Tess" and "Jude." Here his lawless imagination, unchecked by a publisher's wise hand, bolted with him. Both books describe how an innocent and amiable person, after a life of unrelieved misfortune, comes to complete catastrophe. Such a theme is exceptionally tragic, even for Hardy. Indeed, it is so exceptional that the author who chooses it must be particularly careful to make it seem inevitable. Otherwise he will not carry the reader along with him. We shall simply refuse to believe such dreadful things could happen. Hardy starts off in both books convincingly enough, but in both, two-thirds of the way through, his imagination gets out of hand; and to give his catastrophe the required intensity of blackness he breaks with probability altogether. Tess is, first of all, seduced by Alec. Later on she becomes engaged to Angel, who knows nothing of her lapse. After her wedding she tells him. Angel is a doctrinaire idealist, who loves her because to him she has been the incarnation of innocent virtue. Horrified at her confession, he deserts her. So far, so good. It is a painful story and it is a possible story. But now Hardy begins to lose grip. First of all, as we have seen, he brings Alec back into her life, unconvincingly disguised as a Revivalist preacher. Then he would have us believe that Tess goes back to him in order to get money to support her poverty-stricken family—though she could more easily have got money from Angel's relations. Finally, Angel comes back, penitent for his heartlessness and willing to forgive her. She flees with him, but makes use of the few moments before she starts to murder Alec with a breakfast knife: with the result that she is shortly afterwards arrested and hanged at Winchester. This last section of the book is imagined with such intensity that, on first reading, it sweeps us off our feet. But a cooler perusal begins to shake our faith. Why on earth should Tess murder Alec if, in the first place, Angel is penitent, and, in the second, she is willing to go back to him? The only explanation can be that Hardy has imagined the work aesthetically as a gradually darkening tragedy, the appropriate climax of which must be a catastrophe as black and brutal as an official hanging. If he can get this emotional effect, he does not care if the factual structure on which it is built is convincing or not.

The end of Jude violates probability, if possible, more flagrantly. The theme of "Jude" is the conflict between a sensitive, passionate temperament, with a cruel, conventional world. Once more, Hardy begins well enough. Jude, a poor country boy, longs for satisfaction, both of mind and heart. After difficulties, he succeeds in going to Oxford, where he hopes to get some education to fulfil his mental wants; but before he has got there his passionate temperament has already betrayed him into a short-lived marriage with the coarse Arabella. Now the blow begins to fall upon him. First, Oxford rejects him, and secondly, he falls in love with his true affinity, his cousin Sue. She, in order to drive him from her heart—for there seems no legal way to get free of Arabella—marries Philotson, a schoolmaster. It is all in vain; desperately in love, they defy convention and elope. Up to this point the plot is credible; and if Hardy wanted a sad ending, it should have been possible for him to devise a convincing one which would illustrate how happiness—pursued in defiance of convention—is unattainable, and that all the efforts of Sue and Jude must end in misery. However, this was not enough—his wild, Gothic imagination wanted something more appalling and terrific. In his efforts to attain this, once more he flings probability to the winds. First of all, though they both obtain a divorce, they neither marry nor leave the district they live in. In consequence, they are ostracised. Jude gets no work, and they sink lower and lower. This is unlikely enough. People as poor as they are and with children simply would not have yielded to such fancies. They would most likely have married, and certainly have left the district. But, in order to bring them to full disaster, Hardy now embarks on his most extraordinary flight of fancy. Jude has had a child by Arabella, who is introduced to us as a symbol of the tragedy of modern life. Already, at ten years old, his mind has been so impressed by the incredible misery of human life that he does not know how to smile and longs only for death. This unprepossessing infant—"Little Father Time" is his nickname—arrives to make his home with Sue and Jude, and, after listening for a time to their lamentations, takes it upon him to hang both himself and his step-brothers and sisters in a cupboard. Understandably shattered by this preposterous misfortune, Sue and Jude break down completely. She feels that she is being punished for her infidelity to her husband, and goes back to live with him, although his every caress is a horror to her. Jude falls into the clutches of Arabella again, and shortly afterwards dies from a combination of drink and bronchitis. Long before the end is reached, the reader's outraged credulity has made him unresponsive to the emotion Hardy wishes to evoke. How can we believe such a story at all, let alone blame Providence for allowing it, as Hardy would have us do? Once more, Hardy has broken one of the primary laws of the novel. To satisfy the demands of his imagination, he neglected the claims of probability.

We may note, incidentally, that the most obvious lapse in the book—the character of the child—is made worse by a misuse of Hardy's most conspicuous talent—his poetic talent. As in "Two on a Tower," the poetic strain in Hardy's imagination has failed to reconcile itself with the laws governing the medium he has chosen. The novel may present a poetic vision of life, but it must also give a sufficiently convincing illusion of objective reality. Now the figure of Little Father Time as presented to us on his first appearance in the railway carriage is a very poetic conception:

"In the down train that was timed to reach Aldbrickham station about ten o'clock the next evening, a small, pale child's face could be seen in the gloom of a third-class carriage. He had large, frightened eyes, and wore a white woollen cravat, over which a key was suspended round his neck by a piece of common string: the key attracting attention by its occasional shine in the lamplight. In the band of his hat his half-ticket was stuck. His eyes remained mostly fixed on the back of the seat opposite, and never turned to the window even when a station was reached and called. On the other seat were two or three passengers, one of them a working woman who held a basket on her lap, in which was a tabby kitten. The woman opened the cover now and then, whereupon the kitten would put out its head and indulge in playful antics. At these the fellow-passengers laughed, except the solitary boy bearing the key and ticket, who, regarding the kitten with his saucer eyes, seemed mutely to say: 'All laughing comes from misapprehension. Rightly looked at, there is no laughable thing under the sun.' He was Age masquerading as Juvenility, and doing it so badly that his real self showed through crevices. A ground swell from ancient years of night seemed now and then to lift the child in this his morning-life, when his face took a back view over some great Atlantic of time, and appeared not to care about what it saw."

This is an imaginative picture; more than that, it is true to its author's interpretation of human life. The pale, sad child in the train is an effective, arresting symbol of the predicament of latter-day mankind, as conceived by Hardy. But he is only a symbol—I had almost said only a metaphor —not a human creature with an independent life of his own. Static and labelled, as much an allegorical figure as the Giant Despair in "Pilgrim's Progress," Little Father Time exists on the plane of allegory and can no more be transferred to the plane of objective reality, on which any novel, however imaginative, must move, than Giant Despair could. And, in fact, when he does meet Sue and Jude and has to talk and act and take part in their life, his unreality becomes painfully obvious. Here, in his effort to give a poetic intensity to the novel, Hardy has overreached himself and upset the delicate balance between fact and imagination which, for success in his medium, it should be one of his primary objects to preserve.

But over and above these sins against the specific laws governing the novel, Hardy's lack of critical sense makes him at times offend against the first rule of all imaginative compositions. He writes outside his range. If a certain area only of his experience inspires the writer's creative imagination, his first obligation is to remain within it. The great craftsmen, like Defoe or Turgenev, always did, so that their work is continuously alive. Hardy does not, so that a large portion of his work is wasted. It is not genuinely creative. He spent a great deal of time, for instance, writing about people whom he could not bring to life—people in the higher ranks of society, for instance. The chief characters in "A Laodicean," in "Two on a Tower," and in "The Hand of Ethelberta," belong to this category. We can see why Hardy chose to write about them. Such people were the inhabitants of the great houses of the Wessex countryside; and these houses made a real appeal to his imagination, susceptible, as it was, to the imaginative charm of the antique and the picturesque. He wanted to embody his response to them in some story, so he wrote stories about their inhabitants. One collection of short stories is given up to such tales—"A Group of Noble Dames." But there are noble dames in his other books too—Lady Constantine, Mrs. Charmond, Paula in "A Laodicean." The result is what might be expected. The setting of the tales is vivid and beautiful. The feeling awoken by the houses was part of his imaginative experience. But the noble dames were not: he never came across them until he was too old to be receptive. In order to draw them, therefore, he follows conventional models of the "grande dame" to be found in novels of the day. These have no life at all: and Hardy's too are just stuffed dummies of high life—Madame Tussaud wax figures of Countesses and Baronesses. The circle they live among is as unreal as themselves. These are the terms in which Hardy imagined that Lady Constantine's brother would urge her to make a prudent second marriage:

> "You are still young, and, as I imagine (unless you have vastly altered since I beheld you), good-looking: therefore make up your mind to retrieve your position by a match with one of the local celebrities; and you would do well to begin

drawing neighbouring covers at once. A genial squire, with more weight than wit, more realty than weight, and more personalty than realty (considering the circumstances), would be best for you."

Or, in a lighter vein, listen to his notion of the conversation of a society debutante at a fashionable London party:

"A young friend of Pierson's, the Lady Mabella Buttermead, appeared in a cloud of muslin. A warm-hearted emotional girl was Lady Mabella, who laughed at the humorousness of being alive. She asked him whither he was bent, and he told her that he was looking for Mrs. Pine-Avon. 'Oh yes, I know her very well,' said Lady Mabella. 'Poor thing—so sad—she lost her husband. Well, it was a long time ago certainly. Women ought not to marry and lay themselves open to such catastrophes. I never shall. I am determined never to run such a risk. Now do you think I shall?' 'Oh no, never,' said Pierson drily. 'That's very satisfying.' But Mabella was scarcely comfortable under his answer, even though jestingly returned: and she added, 'Sometimes I think I shall, just for the fun of it!'"

This is fashionable life as imagined by Miss Daisy Ashford. Lady Mabella is a Young Visiter.

Hardy's excursions among complex intellectual types of human being are nearly as disastrous. Here he was led astray by a different motive. The nineteenth century was an age of growing self-consciousness. People were investigating psychology and analysing motive as never before. The novelists, led by George Eliot, were doing it too. Hardy was aware of this tendency. He even said that it was not to be resisted: novels must be more analytical. Luckily for him, his practice was usually different from his precept. But now and again he does attempt something in the new style. He chooses what he considers some typical figure of the new age—Knight, a modern thinker; Fitzpiers, a modern sceptic; Sue, an advanced woman—and he does his conscientious best to make them true to life. Their opinions and doubts are painstakingly detailed to us. Unfortunately the result is no more convincing than Lady Mabella. Once again, he was describing people he had only learned to know after he ceased to be receptive imaginatively. Moreover, such characters cannot be fully described through word and action, and it is only through word and action that Hardy is able to give his creatures vitality. Sue is a regular Hardy woman, incongruously decked out with advanced opinions. Fitzpiers and Knight are collections of views, imperfectly clothed in flesh and blood. Hardy's descriptions of their thoughts are just essays on the subjects they are thinking about; their conversations are like debates in college societies. This is how Sue, spending her first night alone in her lover's room, converses with him:

> "'I have no respect for Christminster whatever, except, in a qualified degree, on its intellectual side,' said Sue Bridehead earnestly. ' My friend I spoke of took that out of me. He was the most irreligious man I ever knew, and the most moral. And intellect at Christminster is new wine in old bottles. The Mediaevalism of Christminster must go, be sloughed off, or Christminster itself will have to go.'"

Alas, she was mistaken. Christminster remains; and it is Sue herself—just because her creator persisted in making her talk in this fashion—who is gone from the world of living characters.

Indeed, "Jude," remarkable book though it be, does suffer from the fact that its subject-matter trespasses often into territory outside its author's range. It sets out, as no other of his novels do, to give not only a real but a realistic picture of life. Hardy's tender heart, stirred by the sufferings of working-men with intellectual aspirations and uncomfortably warm sexual temperaments, wished to write a book bringing home these sufferings to others. And he is therefore at pains to give an accurate presentation of such a life. But his imagination is not a realistic one. The result is that the book is discordant. Hardy's intention and Hardy's natural bias quarrelled with one another all the way through it. He takes trouble to check his instinctive bias towards the fanciful. The plot is less formalised than in his other books, the conversation more naturalistic; there are fewer flights of poetic fancy; there is no chorus of humorous rustics. Yet the effect is never realistic in the way Hardy wanted it to be. It is as if some actor of the old heroic school were to attempt to play a part in a modern drama of ordinary life. Painstakingly he dresses himself in the appropriate costume and mutes down his voice to the inflections of everyday conversation; but the moment he warms to his work he betrays himself. Back come the flashing glance, the thrilling tones, the grandiose gesture, shattering the illusion he has taken such trouble to create. Sue shows herself to be the old-fashioned Hardy heroine; Jude's little boy is a figure of wild poetic symbolism; Oxford and Shaftesbury are the old, picturesque Hardy setting, steeped in historical and romantic associations. And, as we have seen, when the story begins to work up to its climax, Hardy throws realism to the winds and plunges, head foremost, into a whirlpool of macabre fantasy.

No doubt it is very hard for the novelist to remain undeviatingly within his range. For most plots involve dealing with some aspects of experience that have not stirred the author's imagination. But a competent craftsman, with a good critical sense, will generally avoid the worst consequences of leaving his range. Trollope is an example. If his story requires him to write about some aspect of life which does not inspire him, he takes trouble to study it sufficiently for his picture to be, at any rate, not inaccurate. Even though it is not vividly alive, it is not so flagrantly unreal as to weaken the aesthetic vitality of the inspired passages. It may not delight, but it does not jar. Hardy had not the skill to skate over thin ice in this way. He did his best to acquire it. Before describing the fashionable parties in "The Hand of Ethelberta" he actually went up to London—poor, simple, conscientious Hardy!—in order to attend some society dinner-parties. But the spontaneous nature of his talent, combined with his simple rustic upbringing, made him incapable of learning in this way; and his picture of society is a mixture of the conventional novel of the day and the rural person's simple dreams of rank and fashion—filled with courtly Earls and gorgeous Duchesses and haughty Dowagers and sprightly Lady Mabellas. When Hardy gets on to thin ice—crack ! splash! he is in head first and drowned.

It must be admitted that he is not certainly safe even on firm ice. Hardy can come to grief right within his range. He lacked another essential quality of the critical sense— restraint. He lets his imagination have its head too often. He repeats himself, he overdoes his effects; so that his very virtues at times become defects. The grotesque element in his imagination, for instance, needed to be disciplined with a firmer hand than Hardy's. At moments he seems to seek the preposterous for its own sake. Perversely enough, too, Hardy is most fantastic when fantasy is most out of place, as in his two unfortunate excursions into the realm of social life, "The Hand of Ethelberta" and "A Laodicean." In the first of these we are asked to believe that Ethelberta, though possessed of no special literary skill or aptitude, should suddenly take to writing poems, and that these poems —"Metres by E" is their curious title—should take the reading public of London by storm. Further, she follows up this achievement by hiring a hall, where, without any previous experience as a public speaker, she holds huge audiences spellbound by telling them long stories sitting in a chair. The plot of "A Laodicean" is diversified by yet odder flights of imagination. The villain, Dare, wishes to blacken the hero, Somerset, in the eyes of the heroine, Paula.

He therefore takes a photograph of Somerset, and then, by means of some new and subtle photographic process known only to himself and Hardy, alters it in such a way as to make him appear dead drunk. He then presents it to Paula, who, properly shocked, breaks with Somerset. Dare's mind was fertile of such unusual expedients. Earlier in the story, he wishes to make Captain de Stancy fall in love with Paula. So he takes him to a remote wood, in which, surprisingly enough, is concealed a gymnasium, and persuades him to look through a hole in its wall. Here de Stancy is transfixed to see Paula, dressed in a gymnasium costume of pink flannel, disporting herself on the parallel bars. The spectacle, Hardy tells us, was so bewitching that de Stancy, forgetting all other obligations, immediately became Paula's slave. This scene certainly illustrates Hardy's originality. No other writer, as far as I know, has ever represented a romance as inspired by the sight of physical jerks performed in pink flannel. But such originality is not a merit.

There is no doubt that, if we approach them in an irreverent spirit, we can get a great deal more fun out of Hardy's books than he ever intended. He could not resist an effect, provided it was queer enough. Nor, even when an idea was not in itself grotesque, was he safe from overdoing it. His comic characters are meant to be a little caricatured—that is the convention in which they are conceived. But sometimes they are caricatured too much. Festus in "The Trumpet Major" is an amusing study of the cowardly braggart who has been a stock figure of English comedy since Parolles. But he is overdone: always he brags, always he runs away, chapter after chapter. Tragic irony, too, sometimes gets out of Hardy's control. It is a fine stroke in "A Pair of Blue Eyes" that Elfride's two inconstant lovers should arrive to make reparation to her on the very day of her funeral. But they should not discover they have been travelling down in the same train as her coffin. Such tragic irony appears as a practical joke on the part of the author: it is not consistent with the atmosphere of tense emotion which should colour the scene.

Again, Hardy is liable to over-emphasise the part played by chance in producing catastrophe. That it should play such a part is, of course, an essential element in his view of life. Chance is the incarnation of the blind forces controlling human destiny. The smallest incident may help to determine a great event. But no author should make chance condition action too often, or he will strain the reader's credulity. For, even if man is not a free agent, the powers that direct his fortunes—his general circumstances, his inherited disposition—are too constant to be diverted at every turn from achieving their ends by some trivial accident. If we are really in love with someone, we shall not be stopped from declaring it just by missing a train. Blind chance must only be introduced in fiction as a determining element at some crucial moment when time is everything, as when Mrs. Yeobright's visit of reconciliation coincides with Eustacia's visit from her lover. In such an instance, Hardy's use of chance is legitimate. But his lack of critical restraint causes him sometimes to employ it illegitimately. Tess's fear of Angel's disapproval, for example, should have been enough to stop her telling him about her seduction before marriage. Why must we be expected to believe that she wrote him a letter of confession and put it under his door, but that, owing to the fact that it slipped under the carpet, he did not see it?

Further, we ought not to be required to believe that so many unfortunate accidents happened in a short space of time. Once again, let me ask you to consider the catastrophe in "The Return of the Native." We can believe that Mrs. Yeobright called on Eustacia and Clym at the wrong moment. We can also just believe that she was bitten by a poisonous snake on the way home. This double calamity does answer

Hardy's purpose by giving the effect of a hostile Fate, driving the characters to destruction, despite all their efforts to save themselves. But when, two chapters later, Eustacia's letter of appeal to Clym goes astray because her messenger forgets to post it, scepticism begins to creep in. Hardy seems to be twisting his plot to suit his purpose. The characters seem puppets all right; but puppets not in the hands of Fate but of the author.

There is another reason for this failure than a mere indiscretion of taste. Hardy insists on this aggregation of evil chances the better to illustrate his doctrine that man is the sport of an indifferent Destiny. The most fatal error into which he was led by his lack of critical sense was preaching. At moments, obsessed by his views about the universe, he turns from an imaginative creator into a propagandist.

The relations of art to propaganda are much discussed today by writers. On the one hand, we find young writers, worried by the painful state of the world and anxious to prove that they are justified in using their talents to set it right, maintaining that all literature is propaganda, in so far as it expresses the author's view of life. There is no difference in kind between "Pride and Prejudice," they say, and Mr. Wells's last blue-print, in the form of fiction, for the reformation of mankind. Jane Austen is just more cunning at concealing the powder of her views in the jam of her art. On the other side stand a group—they are mostly disgruntled and elderly survivors from the age of the aesthetes—who protest irritably that art has nothing to do with morals, nay, that, in so far as it points any moral at all, a novel is a failure. Both views have some truth in them; but both are wrong. It is nonsense to say that art should not point a moral. Every artist, like every human being, has moral beliefs; and since his work is the expression of himself, it must also express his moral beliefs. It is the point of view from which Jane Austen regards Darcy and Elizabeth which determines the form of the story in which she exhibits them, and her picture is all the more impressive for the fineness of the moral sensibility which illuminates it. But of course—and this is where the aesthetes are on the right track—though moral quality may enrich a work of art, it is not a condition of its existence. Without her moral sensibility, Jane Austen would still be an artist. And we read "Pride and Prejudice" not because we agree with its author's view of life, but because it presents us with a lively, entertaining and beautifully expressed vision of the world.

It follows, then, that the artist's first obligation is to his vision rather than to his moral point of view. This does not mean that he should never write with a moral purpose. If his creative inspiration happens to coincide with his moral purpose, well and good. The "Germinal" of Zola is none the worse for the fact that, in addition to being a novel, it is a pamphlet on behalf of the oppressed miners of France. For the spectacle of the life of the mine happened to stimulate Zola's imagination, so that he is able to produce a successful work of art and a successful pamphlet at the same time. However, no amount of virtuous indignation would have availed him if the mine had not appealed to his imagination. Mrs. Gaskell felt just as strongly about the cotton-spinners of Lancashire as Zola did about the miners, yet "Mary Barton" is a failure. The artist must stick to his range, whatever is fidgeting his conscience. And even when writing within his range, he must be careful not to point his moral so ostentatiously that it diverts our attention from the imaginary world he has created. Still less must he let his propagandist purpose modify his conception against the judgement of his imagination. Indeed, his moral views are best left to reveal themselves involuntarily. The artist's only conscious duty should be to the truth of his creative vision. Every other consideration must be sacrificed to it. Hardy realised this. "I hold," he said, "that the mission of poetry is to record impressions, not convictions. Words-worth, in his later writings, fell into the error of recording the latter." But so did Hardy; his practice was not always true to his precept. Like other Victorians, he was a stern moralist, absorbedly interested in working out his philosophy of life. Now and again, undisciplined as he was by a strong critical sense, his moral intention dominates his artistic inspiration. Just when we are spellbound by Hardy the novelist, Hardy the preacher bobs up, and instantly the spell is broken. Tess, a country girl of eighteen, is riding with her little brother on the waggon under the stars:

> "'Did you say the stars were worlds, Tess?' asks the child.
> 'Yes.'
> 'All like ours?'
> 'I do not know, but I think so.'"

This is all right, but she goes on:

> "'Most of them seem splendid and sound—a few blighted.'
> 'Which do we live on? The splendid one or the blighted one?'
> 'A blighted one.'"

Here is no unsophisticated country girl speaking. Through her lips comes the voice of a middle-aged novelist, brooding in gloomy mood on the riddle of the painful earth. For "Tess" is a late book. The preaching tendency grew on Hardy. Alas, as people grow older their imaginative faculties tend to grow weaker, and their interest in morals stronger. Not that Hardy's ideas changed—he would have called the earth a blighted star when he was twenty-four. But in his early works—"Under the Greenwood Tree" or "Far from the Madding Crowd," for example—he feels no impulse to proclaim it so openly. They are the expressions of the same philosophy, but it is implicit. The impulse grew gradually stronger. There is a little more preaching in "The Return of the Native" and "Two on a Tower," and yet more in

"The Mayor of Casterbridge" and "The Woodlanders."
Indeed, "The Woodlanders" was only saved from moralistic
excess by the convention of the age. At the time he was
writing it, Hardy, possibly for personal reasons, was concerned about the marriage question, and wished to show what
a cruel tie an incompatible marriage entailed. He therefore
wished at the end of the book to point out that, though
officially reconciled, Grace and Fitzpiers were likely to be
unhappy. But he softened this in deference to the popular
desire for a happy ending. Aesthetically, it is an improvement, like the happy ending of "The Return of the Native."
The tragedy of "The Woodlanders" is the tragedy of Giles
and Marty; and though we cannot expect Grace and Fitzpiers to be very happy, it is better that their departure from
the stage should take place in an atmosphere of comparative
tranquillity; otherwise we shall be diverted from yielding
ourselves exclusively to the poignant emotion evoked by the
figure of Marty in her lonely, faithful despair, which should
dominate the last scene of the book. But Hardy, for the sake
of expounding his views, was himself prepared to run the
risk of ruining his final effect.

Still, these are small blemishes in a successful work.
"The Woodlanders" was not designed in the first place in
order to provide a vehicle for Hardy's opinions on life. This
is less true of "Tess" and not true at all of "Jude." In
these two books Hardy the preacher takes far too much hand
in the matter, and interferes in the design of the ground plan
of the story. "Tess" is an indictment of Providence—a
parable whose moral is that it is not possible to justify the
ways of God to men. One cannot call it a failure: the
heroine is the most pathetic of all Hardy's creations, and
the book is full of magnificent passages. But there is a flaw
in the design. Not only, as we have seen, is the catastrophe
highly improbable, but we feel that Hardy has devised it
too obviously in order to prove his point. He twists reality,

partly to get the requisite tragic effect, but still more to draw
a moral. "Jude" fails more disastrously for the same
reasons. He says somewhere that he thought someone ought
to write a book exposing the hardships to which intellectually minded working-men were liable, and, moreover, that
that someone ought to be himself. This was an inauspicious
beginning. No artist should ever choose a subject because
he thinks he ought to, but only because he wants to.[1] And,
as we have seen, it took Hardy right off his own territory.
Then, the catastrophe is even more improbable than that in
"Tess." For again—partly to make the close black enough,
but still more to satisfy his itch to give the universe a piece
of his mind—Hardy indulges in the wildest fantasy. It is
not, it may be remarked incidentally, even successful in
achieving its moral purpose. In matters of art, those who
load the dice seldom win the game. In order to prove his
point, Hardy overstates his case grossly. No doubt, working-
men of intellectual aspirations and strong sexual impulses
did tend to have a poor time in Victorian England; but there
is no reason to suppose that their children were particularly
liable to hang each other. Like a charitable institution
appealing for funds, Hardy piles on the agony in order to

[1] Other causes may have contributed to produce the unbridled
didacticism of "Jude." The influence of Ibsen had lately started the
notion that serious literature should comment on problems of the day.
Hardy saw "Rosmersholm" shortly before writing "Jude"; and,
whether intentionally or not, there is a noticeable similarity between
Sue's story and that of Rebecca West. Both are "emancipated" women
who are forced by the tragic consequences of putting their revolutionary
views into action, to admit the compelling power of the beliefs against
which their reason rebelled.

Further, we know that Hardy was at odds with his wife at this time.
And, though it is always dangerous to interpret an imaginative work
in terms of its author's biography, this may be why he felt it his duty
to expose the dreadful consequences of indissoluble marriage. The
unbalanced and uncharacteristic bitterness with which he speaks of the
subject suggests this; so too does the unreal impersonality of much of
the talk about it, like a tract put into dialogue form. Personal experience
must be digested, personal emotion must cool, before they are susceptible
material for the action of the creative imagination.

win pity for a deserving object. And he is punished for it. The muse of novel writing is not to be flouted in this way. Not only is Hardy's story an artistic failure, but his indictment of Providence fails by reason of its overstatement.

Compare "Jude" with "The Mayor of Casterbridge." Here Hardy's moral judgements are under the control of his artistic sense. The tragic hero, Henchard, is not a perfect character. He sins, and his misfortunes are partly the consequence of his sins. His story could have been told by an author who believed in the righteous governance of the universe and wished to show that Henchard got his deserts. Hardy does not twist the facts. But, seen from his angle of vision, Henchard's tragedy appears as the result not of his fault but of his circumstances. He was born with a faulty disposition which he did all he could to mend. Fate, however, was too much for him. He comes to disaster, and his sufferings are more than he deserved. Here Hardy's indictment of Providence is fairly stated: and it is the more convincing for its fairness.

Further, the fact that Henchard's tragedy is presented against a more cheerful background adds to its impressiveness. We are shown a world which is not all sorrow and evil—which contains virtuous people, leading reasonably happy lives. The world Jude lives in is a world without joy. It is Hardy's only book without any humour, any picture of pleasure. Jude starts life as a normal man, with normal instincts, but not for one instant does he enjoy himself. He does not even come across any likeable people, except Sue and Philotson, and they are neurotics. We may note that here the general gloom in which Hardy was wallowing when he wrote "Tess" and "Jude" did betray him into philosophic inconsistency. In them he does not only attack the universal plan, he also goes for human institutions and human beings. "Tess" contains outbursts against the current view on sexual morality, and more especially the clergy who uphold them. In "Jude" Hardy makes an onslaught on the marriage laws and on snobbish dons. These double indictments are inconsistent one with another. If all human beings are equally the puppets of circumstance, circumstance is also responsible for their views and institutions. The unfortunate clergy and dons are as much the creatures of cruel destiny as Tess and Jude; and as such are no more to be judged as responsible for their errors. In his earlier books, Hardy makes this point clear. The characters who play the part of the villain of the piece—Eustacia, Wildeve, Troy, Fitzpiers—are depicted more with pity than anger. Are they not, equally with the heroes, victims? But in the mood in which he wrote "Tess" and "Jude," Hardy is so indignant about everything that he attacks human beings—Angel and Alec, Arabella and the dons—as bitterly as though they were the President of the Immortals himself. And even when he has finished with them, he has some anger left to splash over on to lesser objects of his disapprobation —on the supporters of blood sports, or the promoters of the enclosure of common land. This shows an indefensibly muddled mind. But when Hardy's preaching mood is on him, preach he must, whatever muddles it gets him into.

V

STYLE AND SUMMING UP

I

A WRITER'S style, his use of language, is the aspect of his art most illuminating to the critic. For in it we see the relation between inspiration and expression at their closest, most localised and, as it were, most tangible form. Personality appears in a writer's language as it does in the strokes of the painter's brush or the marks of the sculptor's chisel. This is eminently so in Hardy's work. His style is the microcosm of his talent, exhibiting all his faults and virtues in their most characteristic form. Let us examine a passage. Here is a paragraph from the scene in "A Pair of Blue Eyes" when Knight is clinging to the face of the Cliff without a Name, in imminent danger of death, and uncertain whether Elfride will be able to bring help in time to save him:

> "He again looked straight downwards, the wind and the water-dashes lifting his moustache, scudding up his cheeks, under his eyelids, and into his eyes. This is what he saw down there: the surface of the sea—visually just past his toes, and under his feet; actually one-eighth of a mile, or more than two hundred yards, below them. We colour according to our moods the objects we survey. The sea would have been a deep neutral blue, had happier auspices attended the gazer: it was now no otherwise than distinctly black to his vision. That narrow white border was foam, he knew well; but its boisterous tosses were so distant as to appear a pulsation only, and its plashing was barely audible. A white border to a black sea—his funeral pall and its edging.
>
> The world was to some extent turned upside down for him. Rain descended from below. Beneath his feet was aerial space and the unknown; above him was the firm, familiar ground, and upon it all that he loved best.
>
> Pitiless nature had then two voices, and two only. The

nearer was the voice of the wind in his ears rising and falling as it mauled and thrust him hard or softly. The second and distant one was the moan of that unplummetted ocean below and afar—rubbing its restless flank against the Cliff without a Name."

No one could call this a piece of faultless writing. Hardy says somewhere that, in order to improve his style, he made a study of Addison, Burke, Gibbon, Lamb, Defoe—and "The Times" newspaper. Alas, the only influence I can detect in this passage is that of "The Times" newspaper. It has the heaviness, the stiltedness, the propensity to refined cliché, of serious journalism. Nor is it even an accomplished example of this ignoble mode of expression. Hardy's lack of craftsman's skill makes him an amateurish journalist. He is always getting tied up in his phrases. Do you notice how he says "visually just past his toes and under his feet" instead of "apparently just beneath his toes"? When he wants to state that the sea would have looked blue in happier circumstances, but now looked black, he can think of no better phrase than "the sea would have been a deep neutral blue, had happier auspices attended the gazer: it was now no otherwise than distinctly black to his vision." These are mild compared with some of Hardy's lapses. In "Far from the Madding Crowd" he expresses the simple fact that Bathsheba blushed in these terms: "Not a point in the milkmaid but was of the deepest rose colour." This is how, in "A Pair of Blue Eyes," he states that a young man absorbed in astronomy found the problems of personal life particularly difficult: "There is no telling what might have been the stress of such a web of perplexity upon him, a young man whose love for celestial physics was second to none." Of course, this uncouthness is partly deliberate. His Gothic taste shows itself in his choice of words as much as in his choice of subject. He has a perverse pleasure in crabbedness for its own sake—loves to employ words that most people

would avoid; "domicile" for house, for example, or "con-
gelation" for freezing, or "habiliments" for clothes. He
even makes an adjective of the last and talks somewhere of
a man's "habilimental" taste, meaning his taste in dress.
All this is on purpose; and to criticise it simply as incompet-
ence shows a failure to realise the bent of Hardy's fancy.
Still, he was incompetent too, incompetent in the ordinary
mechanics of his trade. He often cannot manage the
ordinary syntax and grammar of the English language. He
finds it hard to make a plain statement plainly, and he does
not improve matters by decking out his misbegotten sentences with faded clichés and genteel circumlocutions.

Yet his style is capable of greater effects than those of far
more competent writers. Good style is not a negative thing,
dependent for its success on the absence of faults. It
succeeds in so far as it gets the author's meaning fully across,
in so far as it completely incarnates his conception in the
medium of words. Hardy's style can do this, though not
always. For one thing, it *is* a style. His strange individuality
does contrive to imprint itself on his actual use of language.
Even though he uses clichés, the final effect of his writing
is never commonplace. His very clumsiness and roughness
differentiate it from the leading article, and reveal a characteristic idiosyncrasy in the use of language. You could
never mistake a paragraph by Hardy for a paragraph by
anybody else. The distinguishing elements in his personality — his integrity, his naïveté, his dignity, his
strangeness—are present in the turn of his phrase. And
to smooth his sentences out into a polished level of
perfection would involve obliterating the mark of Hardy's
signature.

Further, Hardy had an acute sense of the quality of
individual word and phrase. It shows in the passage I
quoted to you from "A Pair of Blue Eyes": "the wind and
the water-dashes, scudding up his cheeks"; "boisterous

tosses of the foam"; "the moan of that unplummetted ocean rubbing its restless flank against the Cliff." In such phrases the poet in Hardy enables him to rise to a level of expressiveness which many merely competent craftsmen do not get within sight of. His words are the only words for his purpose. I cannot think of any alternative for "boisterous tosses" or "rubbing its restless flank" which would give anything like the same effect. Hardy, unexpectedly enough, at such moments has satisfied Flaubert's ideal of style. He has discovered the "mot juste," the single word which can alone express the shade of meaning he has in mind. His words do more than clothe his conception—they are its embodiment. Nor is it always an easy conception to embody in words: Hardy's conceptions are so intensely imaginative. His words do go beyond his logical meaning to suggest all the subtleties and overtones of the mood in which he regarded it. To the poet's eye he added the poet's finer sensibility to the use of language. Eustacia's "Pagan eyes, full of nocturnal mysteries"; the bonfire casting "a kingly effulgence over Egdon"; the half-naked hill of Norcombe with its "vague still horizon"; Henchard's garden "silent, dewy and full of perfume"; the first description of Jude's son, "a ground swell from ancient years of night seemed to lift the child in this, his morning-life, when his face took a back view over some great Atlantic of time,"—in these phrases, Hardy, in the fervour of inspiration, has struck a chord which sets the reader's imagination astir like a line of Shakespeare or Donne. The same power shows itself in the movement of Hardy's prose—in its rhythm. It also is often harsh and crabbed, but it also is intensely expressive. Do you remark how the jerky, wavering sentences in "A Pair of Blue Eyes" echo the agitation in Knight's breast, his quivering suspense, the fragmentary, spasmodic movement of his thought at this moment of peril?; the movement of the wind too—"the wind in his ears, rising and falling, as it mauled and thrust him, hard or softly"? Always instinctively he modulates sound to make it correspond to the movement of the emotion it conveys:

> "Justice was done, and the President of the Immortals (in Aeschylean phrase) had ended his sport with Tess. And the d'Urberville knights and dames slept on in their tombs, unknowing. The two speechless gazers bent themselves down to the earth as if in prayer, and remained for a long time absolutely motionless: the flag continued to wave silently. As soon as they had strength, they arose, joined hands again, and went on."

Remark how the roll of the first sentence proclaims grandly, and, as it were, impersonally, the moral of the story. The frustrated rhythm of the next sentence, beginning with the same grandeur and then cut short, conveys an uprush of emotion, suddenly checked as by a violent effort of will. Then the straight narrative goes on, in toneless, abrupt cadence, as if it were the utterance of a spirit drained by sheer intensity of feeling. This is language used creatively. The truth is, that two elements go to make a good style. The first is what I may call the element of understanding: that grasp of the nature of the English language which enables an author to write it clearly, accurately and economically. The second is the element of sensibility: that feeling for the flavour of a word and the flow of a rhythm which enables him to write it eloquently and expressively. The first element is intellectual, the child of the critical sense; the second is aesthetic and is the product of the imagination. Hardy—as one might expect—has the second in the highest degree, but is noticeably lacking in the first: with the consequence that a grotesque deficiency in craftsmanship appears in his style side by side with wonderful strokes of phrase. He writes clumsily; but he writes creatively.

II

Our summary of Hardy is over. What is the total impression he leaves on us? A mixed impression. His work is an extraordinary mixture of merits and defects. Both are equally of its substance: they are both present in everything he wrote at all times in his life. It would not be true to say that his work shows no development. There is a development in mood. The masterpieces of his first period —"Under the Greenwood Tree" and "Far from the Madding Crowd"—are conceived in a relatively calm temper. The philosophy implicit in them is the same melancholy philosophy he held all his life, but his own spirit was irradiated by the natural zest of youth. In the work of his second phase—"The Return of the Native," "The Mayor of Casterbridge," "The Woodlanders"—we can perceive the gradual darkening of his mood. By the time he reached the last stage, the stage of "Tess" and "Jude," various causes—the failure of youthful hope and his own unhappy marriage—contributed to overshadow his horizon completely. But this progressive development affected only his mood. His basic ideas had not altered. And still less does the quality of his art. He is good and bad, just as often and in just the same way. The light of inspiration flashes on and off with the same spasmodic capriciousness. His best books alternate with his worst. Indeed, nothing is odder than the way, after he has finished a masterpiece, he will plunge headlong into one of his greatest failures. "Desperate Remedies," his very first work, mingles good and bad. It has one of his most complicated and conventional plots, and it deals partially with the high life which is out of his range. But it contains some entertaining rustic characters, some delicate love scenes and some brilliant flashes of imagination. Cytherea's lonely night in the strange house with the unknown man dying overhead and the tranquil rural peace disturbed by the menacing rush of the waterfall, is in his best manner. "Under the Greenwood Tree," the next book, is one of Hardy's most faultless works, conceived consistently within his imaginative range, though without his tragic splendour. "A Pair of Blue Eyes" follows, and is a mixture of beautiful romantic poetry and stilted episodes of London life, diversified by Hardy's unconvincing attempts at reproducing intellectual conversation. Then comes "Far from the Madding Crowd," in which all his great qualities appear in full maturity. At last, we feel, he has found himself. Not a bit of it—what should he turn his hand to next but "The Hand of Ethelberta," an essay in social comedy of the fashionable world, and, as such, mainly worthless. But this is only a momentary lapse. "The Return of the Native" and "The Trumpet Major" reveal Hardy once more at his most inspired. Two good books, however, seem to have exhausted him. Their successor, "A Laodicean," is his worst work. Once more he is attempting a realistic social comedy-drama of upper-class life, and this time he does not even relieve it by those glimpses into rustic Wessex which vivify the lifeless artificiality of "The Hand of Ethelberta." "Two on a Tower" is a great improvement on this. The love story up among the stars is a beautiful conception : but, attempting, as the book does, to make a novel of what should be a poem, as a whole it fails. "The Mayor of Casterbridge" and "The Woodlanders" follow. Once more we are on his highest level, the level of "Far from the Madding Crowd" and "The Return of the Native." In "Tess," his next work, his creative power still burns at its brightest, though the didactic impulse in him has now grown so strong as to prevent it finding perfect fulfilment. "Jude" is even more imperfect, but still, at moments, inspired. His last story, "The Well-Beloved," has only a glimmer of his true quality. It is the same sort of book as "Two on a Tower," and not so good.

This failure to acquire that command over his art that would ensure a steady level of achievement is of the nature of his talent. It is the critical sense which enables a writer to acquire such a command. For it enables him to learn from experience. The writing of each book is a lesson to the author. Gradually he acquires the knowledge of himself and his craft which enables him to make the most of his merits and to avoid the occasion for his lapses. As he gets older his inspiration may flag, but he can be depended upon to make a sound job of whatever he undertakes. But Hardy was incorrigible. He could only write well when the spirit moved him. To the end of his life he persisted in writing whether it moved him or not.

III

This uncertainty, this unevenness, is a very odd phenomenon. No doubt very few authors are equally good all the time. But Hardy's oscillations are exceptionally violent. How are we to account for them?

The original cause, no doubt, was innate. There was a lack of balance in the fundamental composition of his genius. I said in my first lecture that every genuine work of art is the result of a double impulse. In the first place, the artist desires to communicate to others his individual vision of experience; in the second place, he wishes to *make* something in a certain form, to explore the capacity of a particular medium. These two impulses are behind every work of art. But the relative strength of each varies with individual writers. In one or two favoured spirits—Milton, for example, and Jane Austen—they seem to be equal. Their works are at once so brimful of personality and such exquisite examples of the form they have chosen, that it is impossible to say which impulse directed their authors most powerfully. But in most writers one predominates over the other. Pope, for instance, seems to have been actuated more by an instinct to write verse than by the wish to express an individual vision. Did he not say himself that poetry should be "what oft was thought but ne'er so well expressed"? This is very true of his own work. But it is not true of all poetry. Wordsworth's seems to have been inspired chiefly by the wish to give to mankind his view of the universe. Form, with him, is always secondary to content. Now, those writers who are inspired predominantly by the formal impulse are stronger in craft than in imagination. Those who are inspired rather by the desire to express their vision succeed by virtue of their imaginative quality. The work of each type bears the mark of this disproportion in the nature of their inspiration. Pope always writes well, but sometimes has little to say. Wordsworth always has something to say, but often expresses it very badly. The great writers of England, most of them, belong to the Wordsworth category. From Donne to Dickens, from Marlowe to D. H. Lawrence, the most characteristic of our authors are magnificent and unequal—bursting with inspiration, but liable to dreadful lapses in execution. Hardy in this, as in other things, was extremely English. His imagination was highly individual and inexhaustibly fecund. He had but to put his pen to the paper for a stream of figures and scenes and fancies to gush in a flood over his page. But they did not instinctively group themselves into a satisfying design. He had painstakingly— and with his intellect rather than his imagination—to devise one and then impose it upon them. Moreover, the very fact that the formal impulse played a minor part in his original inspiration meant that he did not realise the true importance of form in art. It is significant that the authors who had the most influence on him—Shelley, Crabbe, Browning— are all more remarkable for life and individuality than for faultless accomplishment. So are his beloved Gothic builders. Indeed, we find him quoting their example, on

one occasion, to prove that a certain irregularity and lack of
plan are necessary to give scope for spontaneity and the free
play of fancy.

On the other hand, all Henry James's mastery of his craft
did not compensate to Hardy for what was, in his view, a
deficiency of subject. As for the Flaubertian ideal of
aesthetic conscientiousness, the notion that it was unforgiv-
able for a writer to let his work appear unless its every word
and sentence had been wrought to the highest pitch of
perfection of which he was capable, it had never crossed
Hardy's mental horizon. "If I had known what a stir 'Tess'
was going to make," he once remarked to a friend, "I should
have tried to make it a really good book."

Hardy's upbringing increased his predisposition towards
inequality. Such a talent as his would never have produced
consistently good work; but the circumstances in which
Fate had placed him did everything to increase his natural
tendencies. His childhood, first of all—spent in a cottage in
remote Wessex—left its stamp. It helped to bring out his
good qualities: "Children brought up in country places,"
he once said, "are imaginative, dreamy and credulous of
vague mystery." Rooted in the elemental substance of
human life, warmed by the presence of nature, coloured by
a folk-tradition, Hardy's imagination learned to flourish with
an unselfconscious strength and boldness impossible to one
brought up in an urban industrial town. But equally his
environment cut him off from any tradition of culture that
might have instilled into him that critical sense which was
not implanted by nature. When he came to maturity, he
made a conscientious effort to get over this disability. Hardy
was a great self-educator; and his novels are marked by the
fruits of his labours. He is always quoting from Shelley and
Plato and other eminent authors. He enjoys comparing his
scenes with the pictures of artists he has seen in his instructive visits to public galleries—often very obscure ones,

K

like Sallaert or Van Alsloot. Even Ethelberta, his single attempt to portray a society adventuress, turns—very improbably—for advice at a difficult moment in her fortunes to the works of John Stuart Mill. But such references only serve to bring out Hardy's fundamental lack of sophistication. Like his propensity to stilted phrases, they have the touching pedantry of the self-educated countryman, naïvely pleased with his hardly acquired learning. Indeed, it is the inevitable defect of a spontaneous genius like Hardy's that it is impervious to education. No amount of painstaking study got him within sight of achieving that intuitive good taste, that instinctive grasp of the laws of literature, which is the native heritage of one bred from childhood in the atmosphere of a high culture. The only tradition Hardy thoroughly assimilated was the ancient Shakespearean tradition, which is the heritage of all Englishmen. When he sets out to search for new masters from whom to learn his art, he is at sea. It is a comical proof of his naïveté that when he wished to get lessons in how to construct a fitting form for the visions of his sublime imagination he went modestly to school at the feet of Wilkie Collins! He had heard that Wilkie Collins was good at plots ; and the fact that his books were only superior mystery thrillers did not strike Hardy as likely to make them unsuitable models for his own very different purposes.

But, indeed, it is hard to see to whom he should have turned for a model. The final contributing cause of his inequality is the condition of the novel in his day. There was no perfected tradition of novel writing in England. The Fielding formula of fiction—which, with some modifications, Hardy adopted—was an imperfect affair. For the compromise between non-realistic drama and realistic picture of manners on which it rested was an illogical, uneasy compromise. The artificial intrigue and stock characters and situations which cumbered it up were so much dead wood, ncapable of being made imaginatively fruitful. Not the greatest genius could be expected to create perfect works of art in such a form. And, in fact, no one did. Fielding and Scott, Dickens and Smollett, are as unequal as they are inspired. Hardy's natural and uncritical talent made him the last man to succeed where these had failed. The death of Mrs. Charmond and the character of Alec d'Urberville exhibit the defects of the form he had chosen, just as crudely as the plot of "Nicholas Nickleby" or the heroines of the Waverley novels. The convention he chose to write in was a fundamentally defective one; and, however carefully we school ourselves to accept it while we are reading it, now and again these defects will give us an unavoidable jar.

All the same, Hardy was right to adopt it. He had not the natural sense of structure to carry him to success as a pioneer of the new, freer form of realistic novel writing. When he tries in "Jude," the result is disastrous. The story is no more probable than those of his earlier books, and the improbability seems far more out of place. Further, when, as in the conclusions of "The Return of the Native" and "The Woodlanders," he defers to the old conventions against his original intention, the book profits by it. But, over and above all this, the peculiar nature of Hardy's inspiration would have been hampered by a more realistic mode of expression. A poetic talent is most at home in a stylised form. It is noteworthy that in so far as Hardy did modify the convention he inherited, it was in a different direction to his contemporaries. Like them, he aspired to add intellectual and emotional weight to the novel, to raise it to the status of great poetry and great drama. But he sought to further this end by making it less, rather than more, realistic. To achieve tragic intensity he turned to tragedy for a model; and to find true tragedy in English letters he had to go back to writers who lived before the novel was invented. Tess differs from a Dickens heroine.

She is not more like Anna Karenina, however. She is more like the Duchess of Malfi. Eustacia is the sister of Vittoria: Joseph Poorgrass, Gaffer Cantle and the rest of Hardy's rustics are of the family of Snug the Joiner and Bottom the Weaver.

Indeed, it is with the creators of these characters that Hardy's essential affinity lay. Here at last we come to the central significance of the truth about his genius, the key to his riddle, the figure in his carpet. This is the fact that strikes us, now that his figure has receded far enough into the past for its true place in the perspective of English literature to be visible. Hardy was a man born after his time—the last lonely representative of an ancient race, strayed, by some accident of Destiny, into the alien world of the later nineteenth century. His circumstances were peculiar. The society in which he was brought up was that in which the ancient mode of life lingered longest. Rural Wessex was still feudal pre-industrial Wessex, with its villages clustering round the great houses and church, with its long-established families and time-hallowed customs, its whole habit of mind moulded by the tradition of the past. Further, this life found in Hardy a subject especially suscept- ible to its influence. He was the typical child of such a society—simple, unselfconscious, passionate, instinctively turning for his imaginative nourishment to the fundamental drama and comedy of human life, responsive to the basic joys and sorrows of mankind, to the love of home, to the beauty of spring and sunshine, the charm of innocence; to fun and conviviality and the grandeur of heroism; to the horror of death and the terrors of superstition. His talent was of a piece with the rest of him—naïve and epic, massive and careless, quaint and majestic, ignorant of the niceties of craft, delighting shamelessly in a sensational tale, but able to rise to the boldest flights of imagination. So far from being the first of the modern school of novelists, Hardy is the last representative of the tradition and spirit of the Elizabethan drama.

The last—but with a difference; for the age in which he lived made it impossible for him to perceive in that human life which is his subject, the same significance as the Elizabethans did. They saw man against a religious background, as a Lord of Creation, a Child of God, a soul born to immortality. The scientific and rationalist view of the universe which Hardy found himself reluctantly forced to accept made him unable to take such a view. To him, man was the late and transient product of some automatic principle of life which had cast him into a universe of which he knew nothing, and to whom—as far as he could see—his hopes and fears were of no significance whatever. The consequence of this is that Hardy's picture differs profoundly from that of his ancestors. The old world seems very changed when we look at it in the sunless light of the new science. Hardy's England may have the same features as the old England; but, surveyed against the new cosmic background, it has shrunk to a tiny ephemeral fragment of matter, lost in a measureless universe and dissolving swiftly to extinction. Hardy's characters may be the Elizabethan characters; but how different they look when we realise that the fierce passions animating them are ineffectual to influence their destiny, that their ideal beliefs and fantasies fleet but for a moment across a background of nothingness. A profound irony shadows Hardy's figures. Though we enter with heartfelt sympathy into their hopes and joys and fears and agonies, yet always we are aware that soon they will be gone for ever, and that behind them stands the indifferent universe, working out its inscrutable purpose, careless whether they live or die. It is still the Elizabethan world, but the Elizabethan world with the lights going down ; and gathering round it the dusk that heralds its final oblivion.

Such a view entails a loss; dusk is darker and colder than

noonday. And, obscured by its encroaching shadow, Clym and Henchard loom somehow dimmer than Othello. Bereft of their power to control their fates, the Elizabethan figures dwindle in vitality. And not only in vitality: Hardy's characters retain the Elizabethan grandeur, but not the Elizabethan glory. For that glory was the reflected radiance of their spiritual significance. Immortal souls, they towered over mortal matter, proud of their stature. How they dominate circumstance! how their spirit rises to resist the challenge of catastrophe! Even the moment of their death is irradiated by a terrible splendour. Is not death the culmination of their lives, the assertion of the victory of their spirit over mortality? For Hardy's characters, on the other hand, death is only the same meaningless and haphazard extinction as must in the end overtake alike the greatest hero and the meanest insect. They confront it with outward fortitude or outward resignation, they may even welcome it as a release from the intolerable agony of living, but always they meet it with despair in their hearts. Shakespeare's tragic emotion is a blazing flame; Hardy's broods like a thundercloud.

Yet we cannot regret his darker interpretation of the ancient scene. For in it lies the originality of his vision. We learn to see the old England as we have not seen it before, just because it is presented to us in the light of Hardy's disillusionment. And what his vision loses in splendour, it gains in poignancy. The tragic intensity of Hardy's work is increased by his conviction that there is a fundamental dissonance between man and his environment, by the ironical contrast he draws between poor striving humanity and the ruthless omnipotent Destiny with which he vainly contends. On the other hand, this contrast could not achieve its tension if Hardy's temperament and talent had not been of the old type. So many pessimists fail to dishearten us because we feel them to be persons with a weak stomach for life, who feel gloomy because they are congenitally unable to appreciate the normal satisfactions of human existence. But Hardy had more than the normal zest for life, more than the normal fellow-feeling for other men. He shared their hopes and their pleasures; he appreciated to the full the dignity of their virtue. Coming from such a man, this considered and despairing judgement on life has a terrifying power.

The fact, too, that his talent was of the old kind enabled him to achieve effects unattainable by most modern rationalist writers. Though he may have disbelieved in the ultimate significance of the spirit, his imagination continued to express itself in spiritual terms. It is striking that at the climax of his drama he often sounds a supernatural note. Henchard's neglect of the weather doctor's warning is a contributing cause of his catastrophe; Eustacia goes to her death the very moment that her waxen effigy is wasting away before the fire of the avenging Susan. Even in "Tess," where Hardy is openly in rebellion against the old creeds, he strikes the supernatural chord. As Tess starts on her ill-fated marriage journey the evil omens gather round her as thickly as though she were the heroine of a saga. And when Hardy comes forward to draw his final moral, he does it in strange terms for an atheist—"The President of the Immortals (in Aeschylean phrase) had ended his sport with Tess." He was careful afterwards to explain that this was a metaphor. He also remarks in another place: "Half my time—particularly when writing verse—I 'believe' (in the modern sense of the term) in spectres, mysterious voices, intuitions, omens, dreams, haunted places, etc. But I do not believe in them in the old sense of the word for all that." No doubt he was perfectly sincere in these statements; but the fact remains that his breeding made him so incurably anthropomorphic that when his creative genius begins working, it instinctively embodies the forces conditioning human life in anthropomorphic terms. The automatic principle of the universe becomes a God—not a Christian God, but a sinister "President of the Immortals," sporting for his own pleasure with wretched humanity. It is noteworthy, too, that these supernatural moments do not occur in his fantasies, but at the climax of those dramas in which he has expressed most seriously his philosophy of life. There is an element of inconsistency in all this, whatever Hardy might say afterwards to explain it away. You simply do not get a dyed-in-the-wool rationalist writer employing omens to increase his effect in a serious work. As a matter of fact, Hardy was not altogether consistent. Though his intellect accepted rationalism and materialism, his imagination never did. And in the creative artist's composition the imagination is a more fundamental element than the intellect. It is an interesting fact about Hardy that even in actual life he could never rid himself of small superstitions: he would never let himself be weighed, for instance—he thought it unlucky.

Intellectual inconsistency, however, is often aesthetic gain. It enabled Hardy, unlike the thorough rationalist writers, to rouse those shudders of ghostly awe and terror that come from a sense of an unseen power working behind the shows of this world to influence human destiny. Eustacia's death, Tess's tragedy, loom before us all the more compelling for the hint of the unearthly with which Hardy has shadowed them. Moreover, his anthropomorphic habit of mind made him able to give a more poetic embodiment even to his rationalist ideas. It is very hard to present an automatic, unconscious force to the reader in such a way as to stir his imagination. Personified, however, as Hardy personifies, it grows awe-inspiring indeed. Aeschylean phrase and Aeschylean form give to Hardy's blind impersonal principle of the universe something of the living, personal horror of an Aeschylean fury.

Over and above all this, Hardy's vision of life gains

immensely in power from the fact that his talent was of the old calibre. Dwelling though he did in this setting part of time, he was yet gifted with that sheer intensity of creative imagination which seems, alas, to dwindle with every advance of self-consciousness and sophistication. The spectacle of the universe, as conceived by rationalist science, is presented to us for once through the eyes of an intense poetic vision. Hardy's sad, latter-day wisdom incarnates itself in tales that have the breadth, the soaring fancy, the zestful, crowding fecundity of invention, which is generally found only in the morning of literature. He may be the latest of his race, but he is not the least. We take our farewell gaze at the England of Shakespeare through the eyes of one who, in spite of all his imperfections, is the last English writer to be built on the grand Shakespearean scale.

IV

My task is done. I have, so far as it is in my power, analysed Hardy's point of view; appraised the capacities and limitations of his talent; discovered his relation to the general trend of English literature. And yet—I feel that I have still not got to the heart of my subject, that I have not finally elucidated the spell he casts. For we do not just admire Hardy; we love him. And this love is stirred by an element in his achievement that is not to be confined in the docketed, tabulated array of his aesthetic merits. Behind the work stands the man, infusing into its every aspect a peculiar charm, a peculiar nobility.

"There is no beauty," says wise Lord Bacon, "that hath not some strangeness in the proportion." Hardy's charm owes its distinctive quality to a combination of apparently incongruous elements. He was a simple man—how often have I found myself using the word "naïve" in these lectures —and there is something incorrigibly ingenuous in his attitude, both to life and to art. He reacts to experience, both sad and happy, with the unquestioning whole-hearted ness of a child. He embarks on the occupation of novel writing as trustfully as an old man telling tales round a cottage fire, so single-mindedly intent on his theme that he seems hardly aware whether he does it well or badly. No one ever had less of the artfulness or preciosity of the conscious aesthete. Yet no conscious aesthete had a more exquisite sensibility. Instinctively he discriminates the qualities which give its distinguishing character to every object he describes; he can appreciate every subtle association they evoke. And he was as sensitive morally as he was aesthetically. Hardy's moral taste is unerring, responding to every fine shade of chivalry, delicacy and magnanimity, and without a touch of sentimentality or self-admiration. Yet it, too, is unstudied; exhaling as inevitably from his personality as the perfume from a flower. This combination of ingenuousness and sensibility is irresistibly winning. It lends a final grace to the most precious treasures of his imagination, and, hovering round every page he wrote, makes his most preposterous lapses somehow forgivable.

His special nobility comes also from a union of unexpected elements—the sternness of his integrity and the tenderness of his heart. Profoundly tragic though Hardy's view of life was, he never blenched from accepting it. It was impossible for him to try to delude himself into submitting to any creed which he could not honestly believe, however beautiful or however comforting it might be. In this, indeed, he was not alone; other distinguished writers, men of his century— Arnold, FitzGerald, Housman—also forced themselves to accept the like melancholy conclusions. Each fortified himself to meet their implications as best he could. FitzGerald took refuge in a bitter-sweet hedonism—

> " Ah, make the most of what we yet may spend
> Before we too into the dust descend ";

Arnold confronted life with a dignified stoicism; Housman with a despairing, romantic defiance. But Hardy's situation was more painful than theirs: the demands of his nature could not be thus satisfied. His tender heart responded with too anguished a sympathy to the spectacle of human suffering for him to be able to achieve the detachment involved in such attitudes. Indeed, all question of a personal attitude was lost in the tide of selfless pity which welled up in him at the sight of tormented mankind. For himself, he strove to face life in a spirit of quiet resignation. After all, what right had he to complain till he was sure he had paid his full debt of sympathy to such of his fellow-men—how many of them there were!—whom Fate had treated more hardly than himself. In a late poem he says:

> "A cry from the green-grained sticks of the fire
>   Made me gaze where it seemed to be:
> 'Twas my own voice talking therefrom to me
> On how I had walked when my sun was higher,
>   My heart in its arrogancy.
>
> 'You held not to whatsoever was true,'
>   Said my own voice talking to me:
> 'Whatsoever was just you were slack to see;
> Kept not things lovely and pure in view,'
>   Said my own voice talking to me.
>
> 'You slighted her that endureth all,'
>   Said my own voice talking to me;
> 'Vaunteth not, trusteth hopefully;
> That suffereth long and is kind withal,'
>   Said my own voice talking to me.
>
> 'You taught not that which you set about,'
>   Said my own voice talking to me;
> 'That the greatest of things is Charity. . . .'
> And the sticks burnt low, and the fire went out,
>   And my voice ceased talking to me."

Hardy was wrong—he had always taught what he had set

about. Only his great modesty made him doubt it. But this poem is deeply revealing. For it shows how, though he could not honestly accept the supernatural sanctions of Christian morality, it still found an indisputable sanction in the voice of his higher self. The Christian virtues—fidelity, compassion, humility—were the most beautiful to him; and the same integrity that compelled him to accept the grim view of life which his reason told him was the true one, kept him also faithful to what his instinct told him was the highest ideal of virtue. These virtues might be of no avail in the universe; they might be born only to strive and suffer and be defeated; all the same, he ranged himself under their banner. Indeed, whatever may be said to the contrary by Mr. Eliot and Mr. Chesterton and other professional champions of orthodoxy, Hardy was one of the most Christian spirits that ever lived. The ideal of character he presents to us—in Diggory and Tess, Marty and Giles—is, far more than that presented by many officially orthodox writers, a specifically Christian ideal: the ideal set up in the Beatitudes, meek, merciful, pure in heart and peace-making, its highest virtue a self-sacrificing love for others. Hardy's very pessimism is of a kind only possible to one indissolubly wedded to Christian standards of value. Christian teachers have always said that there was no alternative to Christianity but pessimism, that if Christian doctrine was not true, life was a tragedy. Hardy quite agreed with them. But he could not think the doctrine true, all the same. He found it impossible to believe the Christian hope.

He may have been mistaken in this. Myself, I think he was. But he can only be respected for the honesty which compelled him to accept a philosophy of the universe so repugnant to the deepest instincts of his heart. And still more must he be honoured for that elevation of soul which enabled him to maintain the Christian temper without the help of the Christian consolation. Bitter and hard as he